A HISTORY OF IRISH CATHOLICISM

VOLUME II

5

The Church in Gaelic Ireland: Thirteenth to Fifteenth Centuries

Canice Mooney, O.F.M.

D1333801

GILL AND MACMILLAN   –   DUBLIN

First published 1969

Gill and Macmillan Limited
2 Belvedere Place
Dublin 1

COVER DESIGNED BY DES FITZGERALD

SBN 7171 0263 7

Printed in the Republic of Ireland by Cahill and Co. Limited
Parkgate Street, Dublin 8

BIBLIOGRAPHICAL ABBREVIATIONS

Bibliographical abbreviations follow in general the list given in *Irish Historical Studies*, Supplement I (January 1968). A bibliography, together with a full list of abbreviations, will be published with the completion of the text of the volume. The following list is printed for the convenience of readers of this fascicule.

Printed Books

A.F.M.	*Annala rioghachta Eireann: Annals of the kingdom of Ireland by the Four Masters*, ed. J. O'Donovan, 7 vols., Dublin 1848-51; reprint, New York 1966.
A.L.C.	*The Annals of Loch Cé: a chronicle of Irish affairs,* 1014-1590. Ed. W. M. Hennessy, 2 vols., London 1871; reflex facsimile, Irish Manuscripts Commission, Dublin 1939.
A.U.	*Annals of Ulster*, ed. W. M. Hennessy and B. MacCarthy, Dublin 1887-1901.
Annales Minorum	Wadding, Luke, *Annales Minorum seu trium Ordinum a S. Francisco institutorum continuati*, ed. A. Chiappini, Quaracchi 1931.
Ann. Conn.	*Annála Connacht . . . (A.D. 1224-1544)*, ed. A. Martin Freeman, Dublin 1944.
Annats, Ulster	*De annatis Hiberniae . . .*, vol. I: Ulster, ed. M. A. Costello and Ambrose Coleman, Dundalk 1909, Maynooth 1912.
Bibliog. Soc. Ire. Pub.	*Bibliographical Society of Ireland* [*Publications*], 6 vols., 1918-58.
B. M. cat. Ir. MSS	*Catalogue of Irish manuscripts in the British Museum*, vol. I, by S. H. O'Grady; vol. II, by R. Flower, London 1926.
Cal. close rolls	*Calendar of the close rolls, London* 1900 —.
Cal. doc. Ire.	*Calendar of documents relating to Ireland*, 5 vols., London 1875-86.
Cal. papal letters	*Calendar of entries in the papal registers relating to Great Britain and Ireland: papal letters*, 14 vols., London 1893—.
Cal. papal petitions	*Calendar of entries in the papal registers relating to Great Britain and Ireland: petitions to the pope, 1342-1419*, London, 1896.

Fitzmaurice and Little, *Franciscan province Ire.*	E. B. Fitzmaurice and A. G. Little, *Materials for the history of the Franciscan province of Ireland*, Manchester 1920.
H.M.C. rep. 9	*Ninth report of the Historical Manuscripts Commission*, London.
Inq. cancell. Hib. repert.	*Inquisitionum in officio rotulorum cancellariae Hiberniae . . . repertorium*, 2 vols., Dublin 1826-9.
Ire. under Eliz. & Jas I	*Ireland under Elizabeth and James I*, [Spenser, Davies, Moryson], ed. H. Morley, London 1890.
Kenney, *Sources*	James F. Kenney, *The Sources for the Early History of Ireland*, I. *Ecclesiastical*, New York 1929.
Misc. Ir. Annals	*Miscellaneous Irish Annals (A.D. 1114-1437)*, ed. S. Ó hInnse, Dublin 1947.
Misc. Ir. Arch. Soc.	*Miscellany of the Irish Archaeological Society*, Dublin 1846.
S. P. Hen. VIII	*State papers, Henry VIII*, 11 vols., London 1830-52.
T.C.D. cat. Ir. MSS	T. K. Abbott and E. J. Gwynn, *Catalogue of the Irish manuscripts in the library of Trinity College, Dublin*, Dublin 1921.
T.C.D. cat. MSS	T. K. Abbott, *Catalogue of the manuscripts in the library of Trinity College, Dublin . . .* , Dublin 1900.
Theiner, *Vetera mon.*	A. Theiner, *Vetera monumenta Hibernorum et Scotorum*, Rome 1864.

Periodicals

Anal. Hib.	*Analecta Hibernica, including the reports of the Irish Manuscripts Commission*, Dublin, 1930—.
Archiv. Hib.	*Archivium Hibernicum or Irish historical records*, Maynooth, 1912—.
I.E.R.	*Irish Ecclesiastical Record*, Dublin 1864-1968.
I.H.S.	*Irish Historical Studies*, Dublin 1938—.
R.I.A. Proc.	*Proceedings of the Royal Irish Academy*, Dublin 1836—.
R.S.A.I. Jn.	*Journal of the Royal Society of Antiquaries of Ireland*, Dublin 1892—.

THE CHURCH IN GAELIC IRELAND

Canice Mooney, O.F.M.

THE DIVIDED CHURCH

THERE were two noteworthy aspects of the Anglo-Norman invasion of Ireland. The first was the rapidity with which the pioneering Anglo-Norman knights penetrated into every corner of the country, winning sword-land, erecting castles, and intermarrying with the daughters and sisters of the local chieftains. The second was the recurring failure of the colonists over so many centuries either to subjugate or to assimilate the Old Irish. It was the combination of those two factors that provided the problem of what came to be known as *Ecclesia inter Hibernos,* 'The Church among the Irish', or 'The Church in the Irish districts'.

The Irish never fully lost consciousness of their national identity, nor was the attraction of their own traditional way of life ever fully extinguished during the late medieval period. Were a national leader of sufficient stature to appear, they would have been willing to sink local differences and forget tribal rivalries to rally to his banner and join in an all-out struggle against the invader. The exhortation of the poet Tadhg Dall O hUiginn to Brian of the Ramparts is fairly typical. It is only the man of war, he tells him, who will secure peace. The nobles of the Gael are being pushed out to the rim of Banba while troops of the Gall occupy the fair centre of the island. Make war on the Saxon, he counsels, and fellow-feeling will cause the five great peoples of Ireland to join forces with him. Then will the Saxon be vanquished,

A

so that henceforth none but Irishmen shall rule the land of Fódla![1]

A description of the state of Ireland about the year 1515 divides the country 'inhabytyd with the Kinges Irish enymyes' into sixty regions, some as big as an English shire, some greater, some less, ruled by an Irish chief, captain, or king who lived by the sword and owed allegiance to none except those who could subdue him with the sword. Along with those were thirty great captains of the English who followed the same Irish customs, being a law unto themselves.[2] Thus, after three and a half centuries, the English in Ireland found themselves little more than an enclave with some far-flung bridgeheads and some scattered settlements now almost over-run by a mixed race of doubtful loyalties. Outside those was the strange and indomitable world of the Irishry, ever a potential menace, yet ever itself under threat from the settler, who had the advantage that in a crisis he could call on the greater reserves and more up-to-date equipment of the neighbouring island.

The most palpable evil resulting from the political situation in Ireland was that the Irish were regarded as a subject race and were even characterized, unless the contrary was clear in a particular case, as the king's Irish enemies. The promotion of Irish clerics was blocked on flimsy pretexts, and they were hampered by all sorts of legal disabilities. In 1217 a royal mandate ordered the justiciar in Ireland not to permit the election of Irishmen to cathedral churches. A document of 1285 advised that no Irishman should be archbishop or bishop. In 1325 Pope John XXII was prevailed upon to reduce the number of bishoprics in Ireland by uniting the smaller, poorer, or more Irish sees with neighbouring, larger, more prosperous, or more English dioceses. In the years 1310, 1336–7, 1361, 1366, and 1380, official attempts were made to impede the reception of Irishmen into the religious houses of the English districts. In 1427 Archbishop John

---

1. Knott (ed.), *A bhfuil aguinn dár chum Tadhg Dall Ó hUiginn*, I, London 1922, 108-19 (no. 16).
2. *S. P. Hen. VIII*, II, 1, 6.

Swayne of Armagh reminded the lord deputy that it was not customary to have the dean and chapter of Armagh represented at the royal councils, nor fitting to permit them to share the secrets of those councils, since they were Irishmen dwelling among Irishmen. In 1536 an act of King Henry VIII ordered archbishops and bishops to administer an oath to those about to be ordained that they would endeavour to learn the English language and teach it to all under their rule.

Like their lay relatives, many Irish clerics chafed under English control, but they were canonically hamstrung. The grant of the island by Pope Adrian IV to the English monarchs meant that any recalcitrance on their part could be labelled rebellion as well as leaving them open to canonical censure. At repeated intervals Alexander III, Innocent III, Honorius III, and John XXII issued warnings to the clergy and people of Ireland about their duty of obedience to the king of England. When time revealed the stark reality of what Pope Adrian's bull entailed, many of the Irish objected to it as surreptitious. Others adopted the more effective tactic of complaining that the English kings were not fulfilling its terms. This had the effect of securing from the popes appeals to the kings of England to redress the grievances of the Irish, and warnings that the grant had been made under certain conditions, which were not in fact being implemented. In 1220, and again in 1224, Honorius III condemned a statute of King John which sought to prevent the promotion of Irish clerics to any ecclesiastical dignity.[3]

The national organization of the church was fractured. All four ecclesiastical provinces, though Dublin to a much less degree than the rest, had their Irish and their English spheres of influence. The unity of many dioceses was also sundered. In theory the amalgamation of the diocese of

3. Information in the preceding paragraphs is a summary of documents, or calendars of documents, to be found in Rymer, *Foedera;* Theiner, *Vetera mon.; Cal. papal letters; Cal. doc. Ire.;* Curtis and McDowell (ed.), *Irish historical documents;* and cf. Watt, 'Negotiations between Edward II and John XXII concerning Ireland', in *I.H.S.* 10, 1-20 (March 1956).

Glendalough with Dublin had been accomplished in 1185, but in actual fact for most of the period with which we are dealing the Glendalough area remained in the hands of the strong Irish septs of the O'Tooles and the O'Byrnes. The growing power of the Magennises had prevented the triumph of English arms in the western portion of the diocese of Down, so that it became in practice though not in name Down *inter Hibernos,* giving birth to the separate diocese of Dromore. Athlone, with its castle and English town and colonized environs, transformed the northern portion of the little diocese of Clonmacnois into a *pars inter Anglos,* but the rest remained in Irish hands. The more arable and accessible northern portion of Ardfert was over-run by the beginning of the thirteenth century and passed into the English sphere of influence, while the mountain area to the south remained under Irish control and was ruled as a semi-independent entity by the Irish archdeacon of Aghadoe. The city of Galway, one of the bastions of English power, was situated in the diocese of Annadown. Not merely had the English of the diocese to cope with repeated attempts by the archbishops of Tuam, who were mostly Irish, at absorbing their diocese into Tuam and so withdrawing it from English influence, but they were confronted with the unpleasant fact that in the western section of Annadown itself the O'Flahertys and the O'Malleys and other Irish septs were strongly entrenched.

In the primatial see of Armagh a long struggle began for control, which lasted throughout the thirteenth century and ended in a compromise. As early as the reign of King John the English settlers in Louth were seeking to gain control of the diocesan chapter and the primatial see itself. They succeeded in 1217 when the first English archbishop of Armagh, Luke Netterville, was elected and confirmed in succession to the Irish archbishop Echdonn Mac Gille Uidhir. Netterville died in 1227, and his place was taken by an Irishman, Donatus O Fidabra, who had been bishop of Clogher for the previous ten years, and who ruled the primatial see for the next ten years. But they were years of confusion and disorder, most probably due to acute racial divisions within the diocese of Armagh. On the death of Archbishop Donatus in 1237 Pope Gregory IX sought to ease the racial tensions by appointing a foreigner, and chose a German prelate, Albrecht Suerbeer, who came to Ireland in 1240. But Irish problems were too much for this German archbishop, who resigned in 1246 and was sent to Livonia on the Baltic by Pope Innocent IV. Innocent now made choice of a Dominican friar named Reginald, who seems to have been an Italian and who certainly was better suited to the task which confronted him.

Archbishop Reginald was consecrated at Rome in 1247, and came to Ireland in the following year. He presided over an important national synod at Tuam in 1250, but spent most of the next six years at the papal court which was now at Lyons. During these years he defended the rights of Armagh in the province of Tuam, and made plans which were to help the Irish cause at Armagh after his death. During his absence from Ireland his vicar general at Armagh was an Irish Dominican friar, Maol Pádraig O Sgannail, who was bishop of Raphoe from 1253 to 1261.

On Archbishop Reginald's death in 1256 his place as archbishop and primate was taken by an Irishman, Abraham O Conallain, who was consecrated in 1258, but died at the end of 1260. Bishop O Sgannail was now translated from Raphoe to Armagh, and ruled the primatial see for nine years. During that time he held an important provincial council at Drogheda; built the medieval cathedral of Armagh which still stands on the site of St Patrick's first cathedral; and brought the Friars Minor to Armagh, where they founded a house that became an important centre of Irish life. Meanwhile Archbishop O Sgannail had been training his successor, Nicholas Mac Maoil Iosa, who ruled the primatial see for more than thirty troubled years (1270–1303), and did his best to hold his own against the encroachments of English officials who were disputing his defence of the ancient rights of the church of Armagh. When Archbishop Nicholas died in 1303 the chapter elected the Irish dean of Armagh

as his successor, but he refused to undertake so heavy a
burden. After a vacancy that lasted for three years an
Englishman whose family was settled in Louth, John Taaffe,
became archbishop and primate. From that date until the
reign of Henry VIII, with the exception of the years 1334 to
1346, when an Irish archbishop named David O Hiraghty
ruled the see, Armagh was ruled by English or Anglo-Irish
prelates; and the diocese became permanently divided for
practical purposes into the two halves known as *ecclesia
inter Hibernos* and *inter Anglos*. The archbishop resided
as a rule either at Termonfechin or Dromiskin in Louth, and
was assisted by an Anglo-Irish archdeacon in the government of the English half of the diocese. The dean of Armagh
was normally an Irishman, who resided at Armagh with
some Irish canons of the chapter, and was responsible for
the government of the Irish half of the diocese. This system
was maintained until the sixteenth century.

In Down, Meath, Ferns, Kildare, Leighlin, Ossory,
Waterford, Limerick, and Cork, the English were able to
maintain their ecclesiastical supremacy throughout nearly
the whole of the diocese and during practically the whole of
our period; but some of them, such as Leighlin and Limerick,
did have a few Irish bishops. In Raphoe, Derry, Clogher,
Kilmore, Ardagh, Achonry, Killala, Kilmacduach, Kilfenora, Killaloe, and Ross, the Irish remained comparatively
free from English interference in Church affairs but were
liable to have imposed on them ecclesiastical rulers who did
not know the language, who were ignorant of, or even
contemptuous of, the Irish way of life, and who frequently
remained absentees during their whole period of office.
Although the Irish, or at least Hibernicized Anglo-Normans,
retained for the most part ecclesiastical hegemony in the
dioceses of Tuam, Clonfert, and Elphin, they had minority
troubles with the settlers, who resented obedience to a
'mere' Irishman and counted on royal support in any
quarrel they might pick with him.

In some dioceses with predominantly Irish populations
but close to English spheres of influence, such as Lismore

and Cloyne, the colonists succeeded in gaining control with a succession of English bishops, in Lismore about 1215 and in Cloyne in 1335. Lismore was absorbed willy-nilly by the more English diocese of Waterford in 1363, and Cloyne by the more English diocese of Cork in 1429. Although there were brief reversions in some cases, it can be taken that Dublin diocese passed out of Irish control in 1181, Waterford in 1182, Meath in 1192, Down and Leighlin about 1202, Ossory in 1202, Lismore about 1215, Ferns and Kildare in 1223, Armagh about 1303, Cork in 1321, Cloyne in 1335, Annadown about 1346.

Sometimes a contrary process was set in motion, Emly, for example, passing back into Irish control about the middle of the fifteenth century. In some dioceses the tide ebbed and flowed, Irish and English bishops succeeding one another, as for instance in Cashel, Ardfert, Limerick, Clonmacnois, and Connor.

The maintenance of discipline was not easy in such circumstances. Every difference of opinion, should it happen that the protagonists were of different races, was liable to be inflated into a racial quarrel. A canonical dispute would quickly become obscured in an emotional fog. An act of ecclesiastical discipline could easily be interpreted as an act of treason if taken by an Irish bishop, or as an act of aggression against the natives, backed by *force majeure*, if it came from an Englishman. Only too often, candidates were appointed or elected, not for their virtue, prudence, and learning, but because of their race and politics.

The religious orders also suffered from the political and racial tensions of the country. Houses of one racial complexion refused to accept members of the other race, not to speak of submitting to a superior of the other race. The orders chiefly affected were the Cistercian monks and the Dominican, Franciscan, and Augustinian friars.

Of the Cistercian abbeys, Dublin, from the time of the invasion, and Dunbrody, Tintern, and Grey Abbey from their first foundation, were communities of Anglo-Norman or English blood and outlook. Boyle, Macosquin, Assaroe,

Corcomroe, Kilshanny, and Abbeymahon or Maune were Irish. Inishlounaght, Holy Cross, Shrule, Kilbeggan, Monasterevan, Abbeyleix, and Knockmoy seem to have remained under Irish control for at least the greater part of their existence. Others, like Mellifont, Bective, Owney, Newry, Cashel (Hore Abbey), Granard, Fermoy, and Inch passed from one race to the other, while some of them swung to and fro according as political fortunes varied. Baltinglass, Jerpoint, Duiske, and Tracton, though normally English, had some Irish abbots, and Knockmoy, though Irish throughout nearly its whole existence, had at least one or two English abbots. King Edward III confiscated some of the lands of Newry in 1373 on the plea that it had gone over wholly to the Irish and that its allegiance was suspect.[4] Granard and Inch, English in their origins and singled out for special mention for their anti-Irish bias in the remonstrance of the Irish princes to Pope John XXII,[5] both later passed under Irish control, Granard about 1400 and Inch sometime before 1513. Mellifont was blamed as the spearhead of a native Irish combination begun about 1227 which became known as the *conspiratio Mellifontis*. In 1321 King Edward II alleged against it and other Cistercian houses that no man would be received in them unless he took an oath that he was not of English blood.[6]

A telling illustration of the break-down in Cistercian organization due in great part to racial strife, was that at the chapter of Skryne in 1496 only three abbots (Mellifont, Shrule, and Bective) were present in person and the abbots of the many houses in the Irish districts do not appear even to have been invited.[7] In 1498 John Troy, abbot of Mellifont, sought dispensation from the obligation of visiting the abbeys among the Irish because of the risks involved and the hopelessness of the position. He had been subjected to violence on a previous visitation.[8]

4. Archdall, *Monasticon Hibernicum*, Dublin 1786, 127.
5. Curtis and McDowell (ed.), *Irish historical documents*, 43.
6. *Cal. close rolls, 1318-23*, 404.
7. Colmcille [Conway], *The story of Mellifont*, Dublin 1958, 153-4.
8. *Ibid.*, 155-7.

English supremacy was maintained in the case of the Dominicans and Augustinians by the refusal to allow those two orders in this country to rise above the status of vicar-provincialships subject to the English provinces. The Dominicans made attempts in 1374–8, 1484, and 1536 to become an independent province. The attempt begun in 1374 was approved by three successive general chapters, while in 1484 the Irish minister provincial was actually appointed. The last attempt of 1536 was successful in law, but too late to be effective before the counter-reformation had got under way.[9] For the Augustinians the turning-point came with the appointment of Hugh O'Malley in 1457 as vicar of the Irish chapter.[10]

The position of the Franciscans was different from that of the other mendicant orders, because from about the year 1231 there was a separate province of Ireland. In the ordinary course of events the Irish element would have prevailed, but two measures in particular were invoked to keep them in permanent subjection. First, the king procured a privilege by which no Irishman should be allowed to become minister provincial. Secondly, the system of custodies was turned to account for the purpose of *apartheid*. The country was divided into four custodies, three for the English and one for the Irish. The Irish custody was the largest and most widespread of all, yet there was only one Irish *custos* out of four. When, despite this handicap, the Irish friars continued to increase in numbers and prestige, a new gerrymander was instituted. A fifth custody under an English *custos* was formed which included several houses in which Irish friars were strongly represented if not actually in a majority. Nonetheless, the Irish friars won control of the province from about the middle of the fifteenth century onwards.[11]

9. De Burgo, *Hibernia Dominicana,* 73-6, 91; O'Sullivan, 'Medieval Irish Dominican studies', in *Irish Rosary* 56, 224-5, 358-9, 361-3; 57, 27.
10. Martin, 'The Augustinian friaries in pre-reformation Ireland', in *Augustiniana* 6, 357.
11. For the relevant documents see Fitzmaurice and Little, *Franciscan province Ire., passim.*

ADMINISTRATIVE AND ECONOMIC ORGANIZATION

For an understanding of the administrative and economic organization of the Church among the Irish, some account of the system of coarbs and erenaghs is essential, 'the like whereof', according to the English lawyer and jurist, Sir John Davies, writing in 1606, 'are not to be found in any other part of Christendom, nor in Ireland neither, but only in the countries that are mere Irish.'[1]

The term 'coarb' or 'corbe' derives from Irish *comharba,* a word generally translated as heir or successor and signifying originally the successor in the abbacy of the saintly founder of one of the great monasteries. By the fifteenth century one finds it applied to persons of varied status – to the head of the secular, collegiate church of St Senan on Scattery Island and of St Laserian on Devenish; to the prior or abbot of the canons regular at Derry; to the rector, not necessarily a priest, of such places as Drumchose in the diocese of Derry and of Cluain-cairpthe in the diocese of Elphin; to a certain family of O'Farrellys at Drumlane, co. Cavan, in which the title descended from father to son; and to a benefice at Tomgraney, co. Clare, which was wont to be held sometimes by clerics, sometimes by laymen. Where episcopal sees were constituted or reconstituted around the nucleus of an ancient abbey, the term was sometimes interchanged with that of bishop or archbishop. The archbishop of Tuam was known as the coarb of St Jarlath, the bishop of Emly as the coarb of Ailbhe. A coarb, therefore, might designate a bishop, a rural dean, a rector of a *plebania,* a superior of a religious house, a parish priest, a cleric, or a layman.

In general during the late medieval period the coarb was a farmer of church lands, sometimes, however, their owner, but with the obligation of paying certain fixed dues and services to the church. He was a *litteratus,* or learned man, able to read and write Irish and Latin and possessing at least a smattering of canon and brehon law. Often, by

1. Morley, *Ire. under Eliz. & Jas I*, 364.

custom, he was also poet and historian, and the keeper of a house of hospitality and of a school of law or medicine or the humanities. In some places the tradition was maintained that the coarb should be a tonsured cleric, who could claim benefit of clergy and have a consultative vote on certain matters of church policy, finance, and administration. Like other clerics he was subject to episcopal visitation. At an early period the custom had already established itself that he was allowed to marry and was not obliged to proceed to major orders. There were other places in the country where even clerical status had early ceased to be demanded as a requirement for the coarbship.

In many territories the coarbship became impropriate in a sept. The senior male members chose a successor following the usual Irish laws of tanistry by which not necessarily the son or any son but a brother or uncle of a deceased coarb might be selected. There was, however, a growing tendency towards primogeniture. The statement that all the members of the septs of coarbs and erenaghs had minor orders and privilege of clergy appears to be due to a misreading of Sir John Davies. The confirmation of the bishop or other competent ecclesiastical authorities was usually sought for the election, but there were places and cases where the right of direct appointment of the coarb belonged to the bishop or to the dean and chapter. It was normally understood that the appointee should be one of the same sept as the previous holder, that there should be no change in the conditions, and that he could not be dismissed arbitrarily.

The duties of a coarb were to care for the church lands, protect them from trespass and lay exactions, pay certain rates and taxes to the bishop, provide him during his visitations with board and entertainment – and, if necessary, a bodyguard – co-operate with the rector and vicar in keeping the church in decent repair, and fulfil on behalf of the clergy and parishioners the Christian duty of hospitality towards the poor, the stranger, and the pilgrim. In practice, his duties, like his rights and privileges, varied considerably from district to district. Sometimes, he paid yearly tribute, in money or kind or both, for the lands he held. Sometimes, he was granted one portion of land free of tribute, being thus raised up from the status of a mere farmer to that of a land-owner. Sometimes, as we have seen, the land became a family inheritance with certain services attached. Sometimes, he paid no tribute at all but supplied the refections for the bishop and his retinue whenever he came to the parish on visitation. In some dioceses there was practically no limit to the refections a bishop might expect; in others, they were strictly regulated by diocesan statutes or local custom.

Like coarb, the word 'erenagh' acquired different meanings according as the character of the office evolved. It is an anglicization of the Irish *airchinneach,* the second element of which is the word *ceann,* meaning 'head' or 'superior'. During the ninth, tenth and eleventh centuries it designated the superior of a religious house, and in some contexts was synonymous with 'abbot', although retaining its own nuances of meaning. The abbot was thought of primarily as the spiritual administrator, while the erenagh was the monk-steward or *oeconomus* who was directly responsible for the custody and administration of the lands and property of the monastery. With time, the name came to be applied to the person, clerical or lay, or even the whole sept, to whom certain church lands were handed over in exchange for certain rents and services to the bishop. The erenagh lands of Ardstraw, co. Derry, and Mungret, co. Limerick, and many others, had originally been monastic lands, but there were erenagh lands in scores of other parishes throughout the land that had never pertained to any monastery.

By the sixteenth century the institutions of coarbship and erenaghship had grown very similar, so much so, in fact, that a casual reading of some of the jurors' reports in the Ulster inquisitions might give the impression that the terms were interchangeable. O'Roarty, for instance, is described as both the erenagh and coarb of two quarters of land on Tory Island. Yet there were certain differences between the two offices. The coarb occupied a higher social position, which was expressed in some places by the alternative title of 'chief erenagh'. Except for the question of spiritual jurisdiction he was the modern representative of the saintly founder and was known as the coarb of Molaisse, of Colmcille, or Ciaran, as the case might be, whereas the erenagh was but the erenagh of Drumbo or Cluainbeg or Tullach Aoibhinn. The coarb's lands were often more extensive and not confined to a single parish. The standard of elegibility was also probably higher for a coarb. The lands of both were in a general sense under church protection, but the coarb's in a more particular way, enjoying, for example, the right of sanctuary. Coarb land was land that in the ancient period had belonged to one of the important monasteries, erenagh land not necessarily so. Donagh O'Morrison is described in the inquisition of Donegal as the abbot's coarb and the bishop of Derry's erenagh of three quarters of land. In September 1438 Nicholas O'Farrelly was granted the office of coarb of St Mogue of Drumlease and the erenaghy of the said lands by the bishop of Kilmore.

Towards the end of our period the erenagh was a man on the fringe of the ecclesiastical state, often though not always a cleric, but, either way, without any obligation of celibacy. The statute of the first synod of Cashel in 1101 prohibiting the marriage of erenaghs and objecting to lay erenaghs was long a dead letter, at least in regard to the first part. The Irish *airchinneach* and Latin *archidiaconus* have been confused by some and have sometimes been used in late medieval times to translate each other, but they were in essence very different offices and grew even more dissimilar as time went on.

In the same context with coarb and erenagh lands one often finds mention of termon lands. 'Termon' derives from old Irish *termann*, modern Irish *tearmann*, a word itself derived from Latin *terminus*. Originally meaning a boundary, the word became restricted in meaning to the bounds or territory of a church or monastery which was under church protection, had the right of sanctuary, and was free from lay exactions, more or less like the cross-lands of the Pale. Eventually the word developed the meaning 'sanctuary' or 'protection'. 'Termon lands' could be used as an alternative expression for coarb lands and for certain classes of erenagh lands, those with the right of sanctuary, but not all termon lands were coarb lands. The occupier of termon lands was sometimes called a termoner or termon man. A coarb was often called a termoner, but not all termoners were coarbs.

Lower in the social grade than coarb, termoner, or erenagh, was the *dúchasach,* a word corresponding to Latin *nativus.* Originally a serf tied to the land, he next became a tenant at will, often the tenant of a small parcel of land allocated for the support of a chapel of ease, and eventually a small landed proprietor. By the early seventeenth century his position had approximated to that of the erenagh, except that his lands were less extensive.

The coarbs and erenaghs constituted the king-pin of the whole financial system of the church among the Irish. They were the bishop's providers, collectors, syndics, and bankers. The mensal lands of the clergy, those owned by them or directly occupied by them, were small, but the so-called censual lands were considerable. The latter were the church lands occupied by coarbs, termoners, erenaghs, and *dúchasaigh.*

In regard to church maintenance, one-third of the cost fell on the erenagh or coarb in the dioceses of Derry and Raphoe, but two-thirds generally in the dioceses of Armagh and Clogher. There were exceptions like Cloyne in the diocese of Armagh, where the rector bore two-thirds of the charge and the vicar the remaining third, or like the parish of Kilbarron in Raphoe diocese, where the abbot of Assaroe bore two-thirds of the cost of maintenance and the bishop the other third. When the erenagh was responsible for two-thirds of the upkeep, it would seem that a common practice was for him to take care of the nave or body of the church while the rector and vicar undertook the charge of the other third part, that is, the sanctuary or chancel.

In the dioceses of Tuam, Clonfert, Kilmacduach, Elphin, Achonry, Killala, and Clogher there was a fourfold division of the tithes. In the diocese of Derry and Raphoe the division was a threefold one. In the ecclesiastical provinces of Dublin and Cashel, probably because the sees were fairly well endowed, as also in the Ulster dioceses of Dromore, Down, and Connor, the bishop at a very early period had ceased to demand or receive his share. They were divided between the rector and vicar in the proportions of two and one, or, if there was no rector with cure of souls, they went wholly to the vicar. The same practice prevailed in Armagh, except for some mensal lands in the neighbourhood of the city itself. In Kilmore diocese in general, the bishop received two-thirds of the tithes of the termon lands and some other lands. The rector received two-thirds of the tithes of the remaining lands. The vicar received a third of the tithes from all the lands.

In those dioceses among the Irish where the practice of episcopal tithing had been discontinued, the bishop received instead certain annual sums from the erenaghs and others who had benefited from the discontinuance. As a further compensation, he was exempt from contributing to the maintenance of the different churches and from some of the obligations of hospitality and charitable relief.[2]

Apart from lands, tithes, rents and services already mentioned, and apart from the stole fees, Christmas obla-

2. The above account of coarbs and erenaghs is based on my own study and interpretation of the data about them in the annals; *Cal. papal letters;* the annates, both those of Ulster, ed. Costello and Coleman, and those of various dioceses of the other three provinces ed. by different scholars in *Archiv. Hib.;* the calendars of the Armagh registers; *Inq. cancell. Hib. repert.,* II, app. 'Escheated counties'; Sir John Davies, 'Letter . . . to Robert earl of Salisbury . . . touching the state of Monaghan, Fermanagh, and Cavan', in Morley, *Ire. under Eliz. & Jas I,* 343-80; Reeves (ed.), *Acts of Archbishop Colton,* Dublin 1850; Alexander (ed.), 'Bishop Montgomery's survey of the bishoprics of Derry, Raphoe and Clogher', in *Anal. Hib.* 13, 79-106; id., 'Marginalia in Bishop Downham's "Description of the diocese of Derry" taken from Bishop Montgomery's survey', *ibid.,* 107-11; Ussher, 'Of the original and first institution of corbes, herenaches, and termon lands', in Elrington (ed.), *The whole works of the Most Rev. James Ussher,* XI, 419-45. For studies by modern scholars see Seymour, 'The coarb in the medieval Irish church', in *R.I.A. Proc.* 41, Sect. C, 219-31; Gleeson, 'The coarbs of Killaloe diocese', in *R.S.A.I. Jn.* 79, 160-9; and especially the series of articles with varying titles by Barry in *I.E.R.* (series 5) 88, 17-25, and subsequent numbers.

tions, mass pennies, confession pennies, and bequests that were common throughout Christendom, the clergy among the Irish had a few other and less usual sources of income. We know that several bishops were reprimanded by the English government for demanding an eric or blood-fine from the family or sept of a homicide instead of hanging the poor wretch for the crime. In the parish of Errigal Keerogue in co. Tyrone, if blood was shed, the eric or fine went to the erenagh, but if the erenagh himself was the guilty party, the eric went to the archbishop of Armagh.[3] Some bishops and abbots claimed 'cuttings', coyne and livery, 'cosherie', and *cuid oíche,* after the fashion of the Irish chieftains. On the death of one of their suffragans, archbishops often laid claim to some of his principal goods, such as his horse, ring, or cup, after the manner of the heriot received by landlords on the death of one of their tenants.[4] The bishops of Clogher and Kilmore claimed a fine or tribute from their erenaghs on the occasion of the marriage of any of the erenaghs' daughters. This was called in Irish *luach impí*, 'the price of request or supplication'.[5] Fines for infringements of canon or moral law, though intended rather as a deterrent and a punishment, also brought in some little income. The clergy were also able to graze their sheep and cattle freely in certain woods and mountains, and to take turf and timber for their own use from certain lands.

In general, it can be stated that the value of benefices among the Irish, episcopal and others, was lower than that of benefices among the English in Ireland, which in turn was lower than in England. Several of the Irish dioceses suffered from a state of chronic poverty. Either there was no proper episcopal residence, as in Clonmacnois in 1449; or the cathedral was entirely unroofed, as in Derry in 1469; or the diocese was so poverty-stricken that no candidate could be found willing to accept it, as was the case with Dromore

3. *Inq. cancell. Hib. repert.,* II, app. 'Escheated counties', II Tyrone.
4. Harris (ed.), *The whole works of Sir James Ware concerning Ireland,* I, *Bishops,* Dublin 1739, 185, 253.
5. *Whole works of . . . Ussher,* XI, 428.

about 1487 and again in 1511.[6] It is not uncommon to find bulls expedited *gratis* at Rome for no other reason than that the beneficiary was an Irishman – *data quia pro Hibernico; data quia Hibernicus; restituta quia pro Hibernico paupere.*[7] The list of lands, fisheries, mills, messuages, churches, cells, weirs, market tolls, tithes and the like in the possession of some of the monasteries was considerable, for example, SS Peter and Paul at Armagh, the Cistercian abbeys of Newry and Boyle, the nunnery of Kilcreevanty, co. Galway, and, to a lesser degree, the houses of Augustinian canons at Derrane in co. Roscommon and at Mayo and Ballintubber in co. Mayo.[8] But in general the monasteries and priories among the Irish were less well-to-do.

The four mendicant orders did not normally have extensive land holdings or numerous impropriate rectories and vicarages. They depended rather on casual alms and on the proceeds of questing tours made at regular intervals throughout the limits assigned to each friary. The quest was made in kind, not usually for money, and by the Franciscans always in kind. Friaries in the Irish districts did not have the benefit of the annual royal alms granted to a number of friaries in the English districts. In fact, when it was found in 1327 that the Franciscan friary at Athlone had passed under Irish control, the king ordered that the royal alms allocated to it should be transferred to the 'English' Franciscan community at Cashel.[9] Most friaries had their alternance of fat and lean periods, but complaints of penury are commoner from the houses among the Irish, for example, from the Franciscans of Ennis in 1375 and of Meelick on the Shannon in 1445; from the Dominicans of Rathfran, co. Mayo, in 1458; from the Augustinians of Scurmore, co. Sligo, in 1454

---

6. *Annats, Ulster*, 154, 222-3, 284; Harris (ed.), *Whole works of . . . Ware*, I, 258.

7. *Annats, Ulster*, 38, 39, 40, 41, 43, 68, 69, 71, 73, 112, 133, etc.

8. *Cal. papal letters*, II, 226; V, 333, 335-6, 428-9; *Cal. doc. Ire., 1171-1251*, 299; Archdall, *Monasticon Hibernicum*, 495-7, 506, 790-2, 814, 816.

9. Fitzmaurice and Little, *Franciscan province Ire.*, 129.
  B

and of Banada in the same county in 1460.[10] The great majority of the friaries of the four mendicant orders among the Irish and practically all of the Third Order friaries were, indeed, houses with very modest endowments.

THE DUTY OF HOSPITALITY

The paramount charitable work of medieval times was the care of the poor, the sick, the stranger, and the pilgrim. It was classed under the general heading of 'hospitality', so that a hospital meant not merely a hospital in the modern sense but also a guest-house, or both combined. The Irish clergy were heirs to a strong national tradition of hospitality which finds expression even in the papal documents. In 1407 Maurice Mac Giolla-na-Naomh, archdeacon of Ardagh, in applying for the rectory of Kilglass, explained that out of the worldly goods with which he was endowed he exercised hospitality 'after the manner of his country'.[1] A document of 1452 states that the erenaghs of Clogher 'keep up the hospitality which is wont, after the custom of the country'.[2] Maurice Ó Faoláin, a cleric of Cloyne, complained in 1479 that he could not subsist 'and maintain hospitality according to the Irish manner' on the sole fruits of the rectory of Mahoonagh in the diocese of Limerick.[3] Again in 1482 he stressed that if only certain benefices were collated to him, he could 'keep hospitality to pilgrims and guests after the Irish manner'.[4] There are several references to the burden of hospitality which the Irish clergy kept up towards all who needed it.

There were small hospitals all over the country, usually adjacent to but separate from the residence of the clerics, nuns, or laypeople who had charge of them. We have references to a hospital for the care of the poor at Drum-

10. *Op. cit.*, 157-8; *Cal. papal letters*, IX, 470; X, 677-8; XI, 177; XII, 103.

1. *Cal. papal letters*, VI, 120; *Annats, Ulster*, 174.
2. *Cal. papal letters*, X, 613-14.
3. *Cal. papal letters*, XIII, 76.
4. *Ibid.*, 123.

reilly, co. Leitrim, of which John Ó Maol-mochéirghe (Earley) was rector in 1479,[5] and to another similar one at Rossinver in the north of that county, of which Bartholomew Ó Fearghasa (Ferguson) was rector in 1532.[6] In 1429 Dermot MacEgan obtained papal permission to erect a hospital for the poor and infirm at Drumcliff, co. Sligo.[7] There was a hospital in charge of nuns at Killaraght on the Sligo-Roscommon border.[8] The annals record the death in 1232 of Fachtna Ó hAllghaith, coarb of Drumcoo, co. Galway, who kept a house of hospitality and a leper house.[9] In 1242 Maurice Fitzgerald presented the hospital of Sligo (*Spitel Sligig*) to Clarus Mac Maoilín in honour of the Trinity.[10] There was a hospital, seemingly a stone and timber structure, dedicated to St John the Baptist (*tech sbidél Eoin Baisde*) near a ford on the Yellow River some miles north of Fenagh, co. Leitrim, in 1244.[11]

The territory among the Irish best supplied with hospitals would seem to have been that embracing the dioceses of Kilmore and Ardagh, which corresponds more or less with the present counties of Cavan, Leitrim, and Longford. To name but a few (apart from those already mentioned), there were Kildallan, Clonoser, and Castelterra in Cavan; Fenagh and Kiltubrid in Leitrim; Granard and Ardagh in Longford; Kilronan, in north Roscommon. Archdall, following an inquisition of 9 September 1590, gives a list of forty-five hospitals in co. Cavan alone, to which can be added two more referred to in another part of his work,[12] but this list should be treated with caution, since in at least some cases

5. *Ibid.*, 650.

6. *Annats, Ulster*, 254.

7. Mac Niocaill, 'Obligationes pro annatis diocesis Elphinensis', in *Archiv. Hib.* 22, 6 (1959).

8. Founded about the seventh century by St Attracta.

9. *Ann. Conn.* 1232, 9; *A.L.C.*, I, 310.

10. *Ann. Conn.*, 1242, 9; *A.L.C.*, I, 358.

11. *A.L.C.*, I, 362, 364.

12. *Monasticon Hibernicum*, 39-41, 783-6. Cf. *Cal. fiants Ire., Eliz.*, nos. 5933, 5935.

the fiants and inquisitions just speak vaguely of hospital, coarb, *or* erenagh lands in the places named. It is to be noted that in Archdall's own similar list of eight for co. Leitrim,[13] the places named are described as having a hospital, termon, or erenagh lands, or a coarbship.

The various religious houses were as generous in their exercise of hospitality as their resources allowed. Rory Ó Camain, abbot of St Brogan's, Mothel, Waterford, claimed in 1477 that he was accustomed to feed forty poor men and pilgrims at the monastery daily.[14] Along with an infirmary for their own members, several of the larger abbeys also had hostels and hospitals for the poor and infirm who came to seek their aid, material or medical. The *Cruciferi* or Order of Crossbearers, a nursing order, had a house at Rindown, known in Irish as *Teach Eoin,* on the western shore of Lough Ree in O'Connor's country. Although originally an Anglo-Norman foundation, it passed over to the Irish about the end of the fourteenth century.[15] Another house of Crossbearers, founded by Anglo-Normans, that had passed under Irish control by the fifteenth century was Nenagh. It was endowed to provide at least thirteen beds for the sick, with a daily allowance to each of a loaf of bread, a sufficiency from the cellar, and a dish of meat from the kitchen.[16]

It has already been pointed out that one of the obligations of the coarbs and erenaghs was that of hospitality, so it is to be expected that very many of them had little hostels or hospitals on their lands and under their charge. These were essentially ecclesiastical institutions and subject to episcopal visitation and jurisdiction. On the other hand, the hospitals and hostels conducted by physicians, brehons, and poets would seem to have been lay or civil institutions outside the control of the church, except in cases where those *litterati* also happened to be coarbs or erenaghs.

13. *Monasticon Hibernicum,* 807-8.
14. *Cal. papal letters,* XIII, 597-8.
15. *Cal. papal letters,* VI, 161; XI, 204.
16. Archdall, *Monasticon Hibernicum,* 670-71; *Cal. papal letters, passim.*

EDUCATION, ART AND CULTURE

It was one of the great tragedies of Ireland, a country so outstanding in the ancient period for its schools and scholars, that that great medieval institution, the university, failed to take root in its soil until after the reformation. Attempts were made in 1312, 1358, 1465, and 1475, but the dissension between the two races in the country was one of the factors militating against their success. The country as a whole had to suffer, but the Old Irish most of all. Brilliant students were deprived of the opportunities for intellectual development available in other civilized countries.

A petition for benefices forwarded to the Pope by a group of Irish clerics in1363 explains that he should not be surprised that those on the list have no scholastic degrees, inasmuch as in all Ireland there is no university. Nevertheless, they add with confidence, the petitioners are not afraid of being rejected on examination, even though they come from the ends of the earth![1] In the spirit of that challenge let us examine the standard of Irish scholarship, what use the Irish made of their own traditional education system, and how they compensated for the lack of an Irish university.

The Augustinian canons, who supplanted the ancient Irish monks in so many centres, paid scant attention to perpetuating the tradition of scholarship they had inherited, while even in the places that they did not take over the scholarly tradition was also gradually lost sight of. Religious communities declined in numbers, organization of the daily horarium became haphazard, the care of souls ousted interest in schooling and scholarship. Since the old *paruchia* system had broken down, local weaknesses could not be remedied by aid from more vigorous communities. Nothing more was attempted than the training of a number of suitable youths, prospective candidates for the community, in grammar and poetry, Irish and Latin, singing and rhetoric. Later, if they showed promise as aspirants to the priesthood, they were taught the elements of philosophy and theology,

1. *Cal. papal petitions,* 467.

with special emphasis on solving cases of conscience, canon law, and the administration of the sacraments. In similar fashion, each house of the new orders of monks that came into the country, Benedictines, Cluniacs, Cistercians, and the lone Carthusian foundation at Abbey, co. Galway, provided one or two masters to teach young aspirants to the order. The orders of friars were organized on a different basis, with more intercourse and interchange between the different houses. There were probably elementary schools attached to most friaries, but schools of philosophy and theology only in some of the larger houses. The Dominicans by rule were expected to have a master or lector of theology in every friary; whether this was always so in Ireland is doubtful. Their most important *studia* were at Dublin and Athenry.[2] The general chapter of the Franciscans held at Paris in 1292 ordered the different provinces of the order to set up *studia pro artibus,* schools of the humanities or arts, for the instruction of the youth of the province. It is probable that each of the four or five custodies of the Franciscan province of Ireland had its own school of theology. Schools of philosophy may have been more numerous. There are references to lectors at the Franciscan friaries of Nenagh,[3] Armagh,[4] Ennis,[5] and Moyne,[6] and in 1438 Pope Eugene IV directed the Irish Franciscans to establish specialized schools of theology at Galway and Drogheda.[7] It has been suggested that the illustrious scholar, Maurice O'Fihely, or De Portu, acclaimed as *Flos Mundi,* may have received part of his education in the Galway school.[8] The Augustinian friars had

2. De Burgo, *Hibernia Dominicana,* 191-4; Coleman (ed.), 'Regestum monasterii Fratrum Praedicatorum de Athenry', in *Archiv. Hib.* 1, 207, 213, 216.

3. Gleeson (ed.), 'The Annals of Nenagh', in *Anal. Hib.* 12, 161; *Bullarium Franciscanum,* VI, Rome 1802, 368, no. 891; 459, no. 1136.

4. 'The Annals of Nenagh', 160; *Bullarium Franciscanum,* VI, 549, no. 1375; *Cal. doc. Ire., 1302-7,* nos. 247, 265.

5. Wadding, *Annales Minorum* XI, Quaracchi 1932, 165.

6. *Anal. Hib.* 6, 52.

7. Wadding, *Annales Minorum,* XI, 57.

8. Fitzmaurice and Little, *Franciscan province Ire.,* xxviii.

a school at Dublin open to all suitable members of the order in the country.[9] It is probable that all the religious orders would have been willing to accommodate promising outside students desirous of attending their schools. The Irish annals contain many references to teachers. Some are described as masters of history, tales, poetry, and other arts; some as professors of music and masters of minstrelsy; some as masters of law, both new and old, civil and canon. One scholar is described as skilled in knowledge and learning and clerkship; another as master of the computus and many other arts; another as accomplished in poetry and Ogham lore; another as the chief chronicler of the western world, and as especially learned in the phases of the moon. Some annalistic entries speak more explicitly of teachers and teaching, of lectors and lecturers. Seán Mac Giolla Coisgle of Derrybrusk, co. Fermanagh, who died in 1384, was lector or lecturer in canon and civil law. Tadhg Óg Ó hUiginn, who died in 1448, was preceptor of the schools of Ireland and Scotland in poetry and general erudition. Uaithne O'Connor, who died in 1476, was the lamp of wisdom of the Irish and high teacher of the arts. Páidín O'Mulconry, who died in 1506, was tutor or preceptor of the men of Ireland in history and poetry.[10]

The papal registers contain references to other Irish teachers, usually canonists and lawyers. Matthew Ó Gríofa, for instance, stated in 1458 that he had lectured publicly in the faculty of canon law for more than four years in the university of Oxford and for more than four in a private school in Ireland.[11] Thomas Ruth or Magruhert, a cleric of the Meath diocese, and doctor of decrees (fl. 1468) studied and taught canon and civil law for seven years in various private schools in Ireland.[12]

Several of the families distinguished for learning, such as the O'Clerys of Kilbarron, the O'Duignans of Kilronan,

9. Archdall, *Monasticon Hibernicum*, 212.
10. *A. Conn., A.L.C., A.U.*, and *A.F.M.*, at years indicated.
11. *Cal. papal letters*, XI, 345-6.
12. *Cal. papal letters*, XII, 284.

the O'Breslins and O'Keenans of Fermanagh, were also traditional erenagh septs and were thus brought within the ecclesiastical sphere. There were other learned families outside this sphere, conducting schools of poetry, history, brehon law, and minstrelsy, providing a trained member in every generation to carry on the noble tradition. They received land tribute-free from their prince or chieftain, and from their ranks in return came his brehon, his harpist, his chronicler, his *file* or poet. Of those specialized family schools, so distinctive of late medieval Ireland and its nearest approach to a university, it must suffice to mention the school of history and law of the MacEgans at Bally-macegan, co. Tipperary; that of literature and law of the O'Davorens at Burren, co. Clare; that of law of the MacEgans at Duniry, co. Galway; and that of history of the MacFirbises at Lackan, co. Sligo.

The meaning as applied to Ireland of the term *studia particularia,* which one meets so often in the papal registers, should now be clear. It meant all schools other than those of university standing, schools that were not empowered to grant degrees, in short, cathedral, collegiate, monastic, and friary schools, private schools conducted by secular priests, erenaghs, laymen, and the brehon and bardic schools to which reference has just been made. Not included were the *studia generalia* of the friars to be found at Oxford, Paris, Bologna, and elsewhere, since they were recognized as of university status, with, however, certain qualifications.

An Irish candidate for an ecclesiastical benefice who had studied, say, for three years at the MacEgan law school at Duniry and then attended for two years the school, already mentioned, of Sean Mac Giolla Coisgle at Derrybrusk, could truthfully claim to have studied civil and canon law for five years in *studia particularia* in Ireland. Let us take a few examples. Bernard Mac Muircheartaigh, a cleric of Ardagh diocese, claimed in 1411 to have studied canon and civil law for nearly ten years in Ireland and at Oxford.[13] Rory O'Lonergan, a cleric of Killaloe diocese, who was

13. *Cal. papal letters,* VI, 262.

official general of the bishop in 1411, had studied canon law
for about seven years in private schools (*studia privata*).[14]
Tadhg O'Mulcahy, cleric of Ardfert diocese in 1473, was
granted certain exemptions for seven years as long as he was
studying in any school after the manner of the Irish (*in
aliquo studio more Ibernicorum commorando*).[15] Another
Ardfert cleric, Gerald Fitzgerald, was described in 1471 as
then studying canon law according to the custom of Ireland
(*in iure canonico iuxta morem Ibernie continuo studet*).[16] It is
clear from the sources that it was possible without ever
leaving Ireland to pursue courses, in letters, in civil and
canon law, that were considered adequate for promotion to
the priesthood and other ecclesiastical offices. Another fact
that emerges is that canon law was the favourite subject for
study. There were several reasons for this, among them being
its day-to-day importance. The period of study varied. Some
did two years of canon law, some eight; some became bach-
elors and masters. There are examples where a person who
could claim only to have studied not canon but civil law
(brehon law?) was promoted to higher dignities.

To seek the more advanced knowledge and specialized
training that was not available at home, many of the Irish
of native stock braved perils of sea and land, surmounted
difficulties about expenses, and faced the sorrows of exile.
Oxford was the Mecca of the majority.[17] In 1252 there were
twenty-eight Irish scholars there, some of whom were of
the old race.[18] From the fact that ten Irishmen pledged their
books as *cautiones* for a loan in 1368, we know the names of
these Irish students at Oxford, all of whom were Old Irish.[19]

14. *Cal. papal letters*, VI, 252.
15. *Cal. papal letters*, XIII, 344-5.
16. *Cal. papal letters*, XII, 807.
17. See Emden, *A biographical register of the university of Oxford to A.D.* 1500,
I, Oxford 1957, p. xli.
18. Anstey (ed.), *Munimenta academica*, Rolls Series, London 1868, I, 23-4;
or à Wood, *Historia et antiquitates universitatis Oxoniensis*, Oxford 1674, I,
97-8. Judging by surnames, William Ó Faoláin was of Old Irish stock, and a
few of the others may well have been.
19. Emden, *Biographical register*, I, 848.

The restriction on the attendance of Irish students imposed in 1413 militated more against the Old Irish than the Anglo-Irish, but for neither had it any lasting effect. Quite a number of Old Irish alumni of Oxford are known to us by name. To confine ourselves to those who became bishops, there were John O'Hedian (ob. 1487); Nicholas Maguire (ob. 1512); Maurice O'Fihely (ob. 1513); Menelaus MacCormacan (ob. 1515); and Thomas O'Colman (fl. 1375).

Other universities and *studia* favoured by students from the Irish districts were Cambridge, Paris, Bologna, Vienna, Treves, Cologne, and Rome. The orders of friars were in the happy position of being able to send some of their more promising students at comparatively little expense to be educated in *studia generalia* of the order abroad, but stringent regulations were laid down about numbers, facilities, and conditions governing their stay. The orders of monks were also able to send some of their young men to continue their studies in some of the larger continental houses.

In attempting to form an estimate of the standards of scholarship attained by particular individuals in Ireland in the period under review, we are handicapped, except in the case of international scholars like Maurice O'Fihely, by the lack of a common basis of comparison. The annals panegyrize theologians like O'Fihely (ob. 1513); historians like Seán Mór Ó Dubhagáin (ob. 1372), and Torna O'Mulconry (ob. 1468); lawyers and judges like Maol-Íosa Rua MacEgan (ob. 1317), and Cosnamhaidh MacEgan (ob. 1529); physicians like Eoghan O'Dunleavy (ob. 1527), and Pierce O'Cassidy (ob. 1504); musicians like Aodh Ó Sochlacháin (ob. 1226), Aodh O'Finn (ob. 1269), and Brian O'Briain (ob. 1364); craftsmen like Aodh Mac Aodha (ob. 1393), and Solamh O'Diarmada (ob. 1443); calligraphers like Dermot Ó Cuileacháin (ob. 1221).[21] Many like Muiris O'Giblin[22]

20. Cf. Gwynn, 'Anglo-Irish Church life: fourteenth and fifteenth centuries', ch. IV of this volume, pp. 73-6.
21. *A. Conn., A.L.C., A.U.,* and *A.F.M.,* at years indicated.
22. *A. Conn.,* 1328, 13; *A.U.,* II, 444.

and Aodh Ó Sochlacháin,[23] are praised for their expertise in varied branches of learning. Augustine Magraidhin, canon of Saints' Island on Lough Ree, is described in his obit (1405) as an undisputed master of sacred and secular wisdom, history, eloquence, and many other sciences, and as the writer of several books.[24] At least by Irish standards, these must have been outstanding scholars. In the case of the poets and the writers we are in the happier position that at least some of their work has survived for our examination. In regard to music there appears to be a general consensus of opinion that at this period Irish musicians were in the front rank. It will be noted, however, that while certain domains of learning were intensively cultivated, others were sadly neglected. Though we can point to many Irishmen of great intellectual acumen, and well trained according to the standards of the time, we cannot name any pioneering genuises, keen-minded theologians, profound philosophers, eminent scientists, physicists, or physicians.

To turn from the artists to their work. The several great codices in the Irish language and many smaller manuscripts from the thirteenth, fourteenth, and fifteenth centuries,[25] reveal the existence in Ireland of an intellectual *élite*, interested above all in law, history, romantic tales, bardic poetry, and devotional literature. The last-named is the only one of concern for this study, and because of its importance it will be treated of in a separate section.

Of gold and silver work the two finest examples are the Ballylongford crucifix (1479 or 1521)[26] and the De Burgo-O'Malley chalice (1494).[27] The crucifix, a processional one, $26\frac{1}{2}$ inches high by $18\frac{1}{2}$ in width, is made of silver, the figure on the cross being gilt. The chalice is excellently proportioned,

23. *A. Conn.*, 1226, 5.

24. *Misc. Ir. Annals*, 176.

25. For the most important of these see Kenney, *Sources*, 24-6. See also references to a number of fifteenth-century MSS in Flower, *The Irish tradition*, Oxford 1947, 123-4.

26. See *R.S.A.I. Jn.* 15, 511-21; 67, 117-9.

27. *Ibid.*, 69, suppl., 14-18, and plate I.

richly chased and enamelled. Worthy of note also is the book shrine of St Caillín of Fenagh (1526) with its mixed Irish and foreign ornamentation.[28] It shows a crucifixion with four identical panels, each portraying three full-length, standing figures. The edge has a stylized hexagonal flower design, and the ornamentation is of niello, cornelian, and spar.

Of wood carving, apart from retables, reredoses, choir and chancel screens, and rood crosses, there are also statues in the round. Polychrome statues were popular. The Holy Ghost Hospital, Waterford, has a collection of statues of various sizes in oak, but only some of them are of Irish workmanship.[29] In the National Museum, Dublin, is an oak representation of God the Father dating from the early sixteenth century, as well as a sixteenth-century *Pietà* in sycamore and a statue in oak, almost life-size, of St Molaisse, which had been venerated for centuries on Inishmurray, co. Sligo. Medieval statues, in hollowed-out polychrome oak, of Saints Molua, Maol-Ruain, and Gobnait, all native saints, are still preserved in different parts of the country.

In the presbytery of St Lawrence at Tynagh, about two miles from Kilcorban, co. Galway, are preserved six wooden statues, of which the most notable is an enthroned Madonna, now generally known as the Kilcorban Madonna. It is three feet in height, carved from oak, and is believed to date from the twelfth or thirteenth century.[30] Two other oak statues of the Madonna of somewhat later date, the Athlone Madonna and the Clonfert Madonna, have suggested the conclusion that 'there was during the early Gothic period a school of religious wood carving in western Ireland.'[31] Of the three, the Clonfert Madonna is especially pleasing in its treatment of the face of Our Lady.

Among the few survivals of pre-reformation religious

28. *Ibid.,* 22, 151-3.

29. McLeod, 'Mediaeval figure sculpture in Ireland: statues in the Holy Ghost Hospital, Waterford', in *R.S.A.I. Jn.* 76, 89-100.

30. MacLeod, 'Mediaeval wooden figure sculptures in Ireland: mediaeval Madonnas in the west', in *R.S.A.I. Jn.* 75, 173, 175.

31. *Ibid.,* 181.

paintings are the *tempera* paintings of Abbey-Knockmoy, Clare Island, Holy Cross, and the Franciscan friary at Adare. Those at Holy Cross are in red, brown, and yellow. Those at Knockmoy also appear to have been in colour, and show God the Father, the martyrdom of St Sebastian, and a symbolic picture of three crowned skeletons encountering three crowned kings.

Two styles of architecture that underwent a distinctive development in the west of the country are Irish Transitional and Irish Gothic. Transitional is associated chiefly with those houses of the Canons Regular and Cistercians that were built in the last decades of the twelfth and the first decades of the thirteenth century. Examples in the Irish districts are the Augustinian houses at Cong and Ballintubber, and the Cistercian abbeys of Boyle, Knockmoy, and Corcomroe. Other Transitional style churches built under the patronage of Irish kings and chieftains are the cathedrals of Ardmore, Limerick, Killaloe, and Kilfenora; the Augustinian nunneries of Killone, co. Clare, and Inishmaine, co. Mayo; and small but interesting buildings like Temple Mellaghlin or Temple Rí at Clonmacnois, and Drumacoo, co. Galway.

The term 'School of the West' has been chosen to designate loosely but conveniently a number of those buildings as well as others, but mainly those west of the Shannon, which were erected in the first half of the thirteenth century. Shared characteristics are: finely wrought and finely jointed masonry; mouldings of windows running around not merely the top and sides of windows but the foot as well; the particular style of ornamentation (foliage and figure) and interlacery chosen for the capitals and the particular pattern of the sections of the mouldings; ornamental motifs of arches and piers; corbel wall-shafts; tapering and pointed brackets; triple shafts and shafts with banding at short intervals; juxtaposition of rounded and pointed arches in the same building, the same section of a building, or even the same window.

The efflorescence of Irish Gothic began about the middle of the fifteenth century and manifested itself chiefly in the buildings of the friars and tertiaries, which show a strong family resemblance. They favoured a long, narrow church, situated usually to the south of the domestic buildings, which, with the church, enclosed a small quadrangle, unlike the Cistercians, whose churches were usually cruciform and were placed to the north of the domestic buildings. The churches of the monks were often two-storeyed, those of the friars almost invariably single-storeyed. Pleasing examples of friary architecture of the fifteenth century are still to be seen at Moyne, Ross, co. Galway, Quin, Sligo, and Burrishoole.

Competently executed figure sculptures will be found in the friary churches at Ennis, Kilconnell, Roscommon, and Sligo, as well as in the churches of the Augustinian canons regular at Dungiven, co. Derry, and Clontuskert, co. Galway, and over the fifteenth-century doorway in the north wall of the cathedral at Clonmacnois.

The buildings of the Irish districts were usually less spacious and elaborate than those of the English districts, but they combined happily the utilitarian and the aesthetic. The considerable corpus that remains, rich even by comparison with other countries, shows that towards the end of the fifteenth century there had evolved, especially in the west, something approaching a school of Irish Gothic, heavily indebted, indeed, to English Gothic, but also borrowing from other sources, native and foreign, and capable of applying the lessons learned in a characteristic and pleasing manner of its own.[32]

PREACHING

The next section, on devotional literature, will deal with sermons and sermon materials. This seeks to summarize the little we know about preachers and their preaching.

32. For the two best general surveys of the Irish ecclesiastical architecture of the periods with which we are here concerned see Champneys, *Irish ecclesiastical architecture,* London and Dublin 1910, and Leask, *Irish churches and monastic buildings,* II, Dundalk 1958; III, 1960.

Complaints about the neglect of preaching and the dearth of trained and zealous preachers are fairly common, and a critic of the Irish scene on the eve of the reformation singles out the mendicant friars as the only group among the clergy who continued to preach the word of God.[1]

An English Franciscan who lived for some time in Ireland in the second half of the thirteenth century tells of a preaching tour in Ulster undertaken by a Friar Duncan and his companion, who was a very famous preacher, and of the success that attended it.[2] He also gives a Latin summary of a dramatic sermon preached by the Franciscan Thomas O'Quinn in the diocese of Clonfert during a preaching tour in Connacht. A terrible pestilence was raging in the district, and people were seeing frightful visions of demons in the air. Those who saw the visions fell ill, and many died miserably. O'Quinn restored the people's faith by his preaching and by his open challenge to the demons to appear before him and do their worst against him. From that moment, we are told, the pestilence ceased and the demons were never seen again.[3]

The *Annals of Ulster* record the death in 1492 of Aonghas Mac an Ultaigh, O.F.M., a famous preacher, and of Donal O'Fallon, O.F.M., bishop of Derry, a successful, industrious preacher throughout Ireland for thirty years.[4] Father Brian Gray (Magrath?), who died in 1549, is described as a celebrated preacher of the Franciscan friary of Donegal, who on one occasion was summoned a hundred and fifty miles to preach before the viceroy.[5]

Nicholas Maguire, who was appointed bishop of Leighlin in 1490, was noted among the Irish for his learning and assiduity in preaching, and a successor of his, Maurice

1. *S.P. Hen. VIII*, II, 15-16.

2. *Liber exemplorum ad usum praedicantium*, ed. Little, Aberdeen 1908, 98.

3. *Ibid.*, 85-6.

4. *A.U.*, III, 364, 450. These same annals describe O'Fallon elsewhere (III, 304) as the preacher who rendered the greatest service to Irishmen since Patrick was in Ireland.

5. Cf. Jennings (ed.), 'Brussels MS 3947: Donatus Moneyus, de provincia Hiberniae S. Francisci', in *Anal. Hib.* 6, 46.

O'Doran, is praised for his eloquence in preaching.[6] The *Annals of the Four Masters* describe Thomas MacBrady, bishop of Kilmore, who died in 1511, as 'a luminous lamp, that enlightened the laity and clergy by instruction and preaching'.[7] The same annals narrate about Tuathal Balbh O'Gallagher (ob. 1541), one of the most valiant warriors of Tyrconnell, that, when obliged to go to war, he always tried to avoid bloodshed and took his enemies prisoner rather than killing them. This was because of the impression made on him by a sermon condemning homicide which he had heard in the Franciscan friary of Donegal.[8] That must have been a wonderful sermon which Tadhg O'Donoghue preached at Cloch-chorr, co. Fermanagh, on the feast of St Lawrence the martyr in 1454, when it merited special mention by one of the scribes of the *Annals of Ulster* because it was the talk of so many people.[9]

DEVOTIONAL LITERATURE

The Irish scholar of the close of the twelfth century who was interested in devotional literature had at his disposal the Bible, the writings of the fathers, lives of the saints, hymns, summaries of theology, and, from his own Irish church, lives of Irish saints, Irish festologies, hymns, litanies, sermons, prayers, and legends. To this collection, late medieval Europe added many popular treatises like *Meditationes vitae Christi, De contemptu mundi, Legenda aurea,* and *Speculum historiale,* along with more lives of saints, hymns, legends, and *exempla*.

From the library catalogues of the Franciscan friary at Youghal in 1491[1] and of Gerald Fitzgerald, eighth earl of Kildare, of the same period,[2] and from certain manuscripts

6. Dowling 'Annales breves Hiberniae', in *The annals of Ireland,* Ir. Arch. Soc., Dublin 1849, 32, 34.
7. *A.F.M.,* V, 1308.
8. *A.F.M.,* V, 1462.
9. *A.U.,* III, 182.
1. Coleman, 'A medieval Irish monastic library catalogue', in *Bibliog. Soc. Ire. Pub.,* II, no. 6, 111-20.
2. *H.M.C. rep.* 9, part 2, app., 288-9.

now preserved in Trinity College, Dublin, such as the four-teenth-century one that formerly belonged to the Victorine canons regular of St Thomas, Dublin,[3] and the fifteenth-century one that once belonged to the Franciscan friary of Ennis or Quin,[4] we know that such texts as we have men-tioned circulated in late medieval Ireland. And such cata-logues and manuscripts reveal the stages by which English and continental works found their way through Dublin, Youghal, and the English Pale, from the libraries of the nobles and the monks and friars into the learned homes and presbyteries and religious houses of Connacht and Ulster, to be copied and translated into Irish. It is interesting to note that the co. Clare Franciscan manuscript contains Latin texts that resemble the particular versions of them to be found in Irish translations and, secondly, that the Irish texts in it are translations of Latin texts to be found in this and kindred Latin manuscripts then circulating in Ireland.

Of the prose translation literature, the most popular text was *Smaointe beatha Chríost,* translated in the middle of the fifteenth century by Tomás Gruama Ó Bruacháin (a name often anglicized Banks), a choral canon of Killala.[5] It occurs whole or in part in thirty-two manuscripts and continued to be re-copied by hand down to the last century. It is a transla-tion of the well-known *Meditationes vitae Christi,* formerly attributed to St Bonaventure, but more probably by Joannes de Caulibus of San Gimignano. Two other Irish translations that greatly resemble it are Innocent III's *De contemptu mundi* or *De miseria humanae conditionis,* translated in 1443 by William MacGivney of Breffny while recovering from a sword wound,[6] and *Vita rhythmica beatae Mariae virginis,* often briefly entitled *Beatha Mhuire* in Irish.[7]

---

3. See *T.C.D. cat. MSS,* no. 97.

4. *Ibid.,* nos. 667, 1699; *T.C.D. cat. Ir. MSS,* no. 1699.

5. *Smaointe beatha Chríost,* ed. Ó Maonaigh, Dublin 1944.

6. *An Irish version of Innocent III's 'De contemptu mundi',* ed. Geary, Washington 1931.

7. No full critical edition has yet appeared. For partial editions see Byrne in *Irish Monthly* 54, and *Beatha Mhuire,* ed. Ó Domhnaill, Dublin 1926.

Another fifteenth-century translation from the Latin is *Instructio pie vivendi et superna meditandi,* of which only a single manuscript has survived.[8] The original would seem to have been written for a Cistercian nun. It contains sections on the control of the senses, conduct in oratory, cloister, chapter, refectory, dormitory, and infirmary, as well as when travelling outside the convent.

Two tracts on the passion that had a popular vogue are the Pseudo-Anselmus, *Dialogus de passione Christi* and a text that is usually attributed to St Bernard, *Liber de passione Christi et doloribus et planctibus matris ejus.* The translator of the Pseudo-Anselmus was Seán O'Connor of Roscommon. It has been suggested that the second work was also done by him.[9] He may also be the translator of some short tracts on confession, communion, extreme unction, and the twelve articles of the faith, that occur in several fifteenth-century manuscripts.[10]

Only about five other translators from Latin into Irish are known to us by name – Philip O'Daly, Augustine Magraidhin, Enóg Ó Giolláin, Ciothruadh Ó Finnghaill, and perhaps William Mac an Leagha (Lee).

O'Daly, a Premonstratensian canon of either Lough Key or Lough Oughter, translated the life of St Margaret in a style reminiscent of the heroic and romantic tales, even to the point of inserting quatrains at intervals in the prose text.[11] Magraidhin, an Augustinian canon regular of Saints' Island on Lough Ree, who died in 1405, translated the life of St John the Evangelist which occurs in the *Liber Flavus Fergusiorum,*[12] and it has been suggested[13] that he was also

---

8. *Instructio pie vivendi et superna meditandi,* ed. MacKechnie, 2 vols., Ir. Texts Soc., London 1933, 1946.

9. Flower, *The Irish tradition,* 127.

10. See *B.M. cat. Ir. MSS,* II, 532-3; *R.I.A. cat. Ir. MSS,* 1256, 1261-2.

11. It occurs in a large number of manuscripts but with widely differing readings. See Plummer, *Miscellanea hagiographica Hibernica,* Brussels 1925, 264.

12. Ed. Mac Niocaill, in *Éigse* 7, 248-53; and cf. *ibid.* 8, 222-30, for what may be part of the same life.

13. Cf. Valkenburg, in *Comhar,* Jan. 1951, 25, 30-1.

the translator of St Thomas's *Adoro Te devote*[14] in the same manuscript. Ó Giolláin translated the life of St Catherine of Alexandria in *Leabhar Chlainne Suibhne* and seems to have been aided by the scribe Ó Finnghaill of Tory Island, who flourished about 1513.[15] The lives of St John and St Catherine are also translated in a flowery, alliterative, assonantal style, and Catherine, here called *Cater Fhíona* is given, rather unrealistically, a hymn of eighty lines to chant while her persecutors are attempting to burn her alive!

Mac an Leagha was one of the most prolific scribes of fifteenth-century Ireland, but there is evidence to suggest that he was not content to be merely a scribe, that he was also a translator and a poet. It is thought that he may have translated from the English the life of St Mary of Egypt to be found in British Museum Add. MS 30512[16] and may have composed the poem *Áilim an triúr,* 'I beseech the Three',[17] an invocatory poem of thirteen quatrains of short lines preserved in the same manuscript.

For most of the religious translation literature we are indebted to nameless men. This is often the result of accident, because of the mutilation of manuscripts and the like, but sometimes because the translators had no other motive than their own devotion and the spiritual welfare of their neighbour. The reward they asked was a prayer from their readers:

Cach aen léigfes lebar lán
agus éistfes senadh sír
Tabrad bendachtain co mbuaid
ar anmain in truaig do sgríb.[18]

14. Ed. Mac Niocaill, in *Éigse* 8, 135-7.

15. Ed. Mac Niocaill, in *Éigse* 8, 231-6.

16. Quin (ed.), in *Stair Ercuil ocus a bás,* Ir. Texts Soc., Dublin 1939, p. xl.

17. Mac Niocaill, in *Éigse* 8, 133-4, where an edition of the poem will be found.

18. An Irish quatrain quoted from a MS in the Bibliothèque Nationale, Paris, by Donahue (ed.), *The testament of Mary,* New York 1942, 3:
    Everyone who shall read a full book
    And listen to a lengthy poem
    Let him wish blessing and victory
    On the soul of the poor wretch who wrote it.

Among anonymous translations from Latin are the *Liber scintillarum* and the *Visio Sancti Pauli*. The *Liber* is an anthology of quotations on moral subjects compiled about the year 700 by Defensor, a monk of Ligugé near Vienne in France. The *Visio,* a text purporting to give an account of the pains of hell, is apocryphal and fantastic but was probably inspired by 2 *Cor.* 12:2-4. It had an immense influence on the vision literature of the Middle Ages. Two independent Irish translations were made,[19] while a similar vision of hell by St Michael, Our Lady, and the Apostles is described in the final episode of the Irish versions of the *Dormitio Mariae* or *Transitus Mariae,* known in Irish as *Tiomna Mhuire* and *Ughacht Mhuire,* that is, 'The testament of Mary'.[20]

This Marian text gives an account of how Christ returned to earth for his blessed mother forty-seven years after his ascension and of her dormition and her assumption into heaven. The American editor of the Irish translation points out that it resembles in several of its features an early Syriac version. The fourth part of the *Vita rhythmica,* which has already been mentioned, deals with the same subject and often appears in the manuscripts separate from the other three parts, but it is a translation of a totally different work. Other translations of Marian texts are *Saltair Mhuire* or the *Mary Psalter;* the 'Maria' section of the *Manipulus florum;* and the different 'Mary miracles'.

There are at least fragmentary translations of *Speculum peccatoris* (*Spéacláir an Pheacaigh*), a work falsely attributed to St Augustine; of the *Stimulus amoris* (*An bhroid ghrádha*) of James of Milan, O.F.M.; and of the *Breviloquium* of St Bonaventure; while many extracts suitable to point a moral are translated from medieval bestiaries, lapidaries, and *libri exemplorum*. Several of the homilies in the Rennes Irish manuscript,[21] part of which was written in 1472 in the Franciscan friary of Kilcrea, co. Cork, are translations. That

19. Ed. Caerwyn Williams, in *Éigse* 6, 127-34.
20. Ed. Donahue: see above, note 18.
21. For description of this MS see Dottin, in *Revue Celtique* 15, 79-91.

on the resurrection, for example, was composed by St Bonaventure.

Among other works that found their way into Irish are the legend of the finding of the holy cross; accounts of the martyrdom of the different apostles, of St Lawrence the Deacon, of St Juliana (feast, February 16), and of Saints Curiacus and Julitta (feast, June 16), as well as the lives of St Alexis and of several other foreign saints. *Teagasc a timcheall na neitheadh saoghalta* is a translation of a letter entitled *De cura rei familiaris* giving advice on clothes, women, servants, entertainers, and friends. It has been incorrectly ascribed to St Bernard. There are also translations of the texts known as the *Twelve golden Fridays,* the *Fifteen Our Fathers,* and the *Nine answers* or *Nine points.*

The texts known as the *Charter of Christ* or *Charter of peace* and the *Harrowing of Hell*[22] are exceptional in that, like one of the two lives of St Mary of Egypt, already mentioned, they were translated not from Latin but from English. There is, however, another translation of the *Harrowing of Hell* which may have been translated from Latin. In fact, there are examples in Irish not merely of different translations of the same original devotional text but of different translations of different versions of it.

John Bale, who was appointed Protestant bishop of Ossory in 1553, tells that Archbishop Richard Fitzralph of Armagh (1346-60) hid a copy of the New Testament in Irish, translated perhaps by himself, in a wall of the cathedral at Armagh and that it was discovered there during repairs effected in the year 1530. The story as told by Bale sounds apocryphal and rather like a sniper's shot in the religious controversies of the sixteenth century. John Fox in his *Acts of the martyrs* also considered that Fitzralph was the author of a translation of the scriptures into Irish, of which certain trustworthy Englishmen, as they informed him, had seen ancient copies. Ussher,

22. For ed. of the *Charter* from three fifteenth-century MSS accompanied by Middle English original, see Mac Niocaill in *Éigse* 8, 204-21; for ed. of the *Harrowing* from one MS with transcripts from two others, see Caerwyn Williams, in *Études Celtiques* 9, 44-78.

after quoting Bale and Fox, adds that fragments of such translations existed in various places in his own time.[23] The *Annals of Connacht* record that Urard or Erard O'Mulconry, ollav of Síol Mhuirí in general learning and poetry, who died in 1482, translated part of the scriptures from Latin into Irish.[24] There is now no trace of O'Mulconry's translation or of the one alleged to have been done by Fitzralph, but it is worth noting that even the reader ignorant of Latin would have had a considerable amount of scripture reading at his disposal, what with paraphrases, quotations, and translations of canticles, proverbs, and narrative pieces.

A claim to being original compositions of sorts, as distinguished from translations, could possibly be established for the homily on the commandments in the *Leabhar breac,*[25] which has been tentatively dated to the thirteenth century, and for a kind of homily on Our Lady, consisting mainly of a string of quotations from the fathers and theologians, which occurs in several fifteenth-century manuscripts.[26] There is a short tract in the *Liber Flavus Fergusiorum* entitled 'The seven Our Fathers which the anchorite Fearghal brought from heaven to save his sister and all the seed of Adam'. It would seem to be a compilation of an Irish author of the late medieval period.[27] Lives of saints like sermons being a form of composition in which plagiarism is commonplace, it is not easy to prove originality. The life of St Lasar may have been compiled in late medieval times. The lives of St George and of Longinus in fifteenth-century Irish appear to be re-tellings of ancient Irish lives. A very large number of foreign saints' lives in Irish can be traced to the works of two Italian hagio-

23. *Whole works of . . . Ussher,* XII, 345.

24. '*fer ro inntaí blad don Sgribtuir a Laidin a nGaidilc*' – *Ann. Conn.,* 1482, 3. *A.L.C.* do not give this obit. *A.F.M.* give his obit but do not refer to this translation.

25. Atkinson (ed.), *The passions and homilies from the Leabhar Breac,* Todd Lect. Ser., Dublin 1887, 245-59.

26. E.g., B.M. Add. MSS 11809, 30512; Bodleian, Oxford, B. 513; R.I.A. MSS 3 B 22; 24 P 1; Rennes Ir. MS.

27. See Grosjean, 'Les prières de l'anachorète Fergal', in *Études Celtiques* 2, 282-3.

graphers, Giacomo da Varaggio, O.P. (1230-98), compiler of the *Legenda aurea,* and the humanist, Bonino Mombrizio (1424-82), compiler of the *Sanctuarium.*

The only saint's life of the period whose originality can be established is that of St Columcille, for which we are indebted to a chieftain of Tyrconnell, Manus O'Donnell, and the scholars he engaged.[28] It was compiled in 1532 in the castle of Port-na-dtrí-namhad, co. Donegal. A large and comprehensive work, it is written in a direct, pleasing style, and is based on Adamnan's life, an old Irish life, various old and middle Irish poems, incidents narrated in the lives of other saints, the far-fetched voyage tale, *Seachrán chléireach Choluim-Chille,* 'The wanderings of Columcille's clerics', and other similar heroic and romantic tales, and on a mass of folk traditions.

Turning from prose to poetry, we find that original compositions instead of being the exception are the rule. The chief religious poets of the period were Donnchadh Mór Ó Dálaigh, who died in 1244, 'a master of poetry who has never been excelled and never will be,' according to the *Annals of Connacht;*[29] secondly, Pilib Bocht Ó hUiginn, who died in 1487, called in the *Annals of Ulster,* 'the best and greatest religious poet in these latter times';[30] and thirdly, Tadhg Óg Ó hUiginn, who died in 1448, described in the same annals[31] as the preceptor of the schools of Ireland and Scotland in poetry and learning and as the keeper of a general house of hospitality.

In the general index to the catalogue of the Royal Irish Academy are listed about 150 poems attributed to Donnchadh Mór. Many or most of those attributions are false, but their number is a tribute to his prestige. A poem with an interesting theme that is almost certainly his is

---

28. O'Kelleher and Schoepperle (ed.), *Betha Colaim Chille,* Urbana (Illinois) 1918.

29. *Ann. Conn.,* 1244, 7.

30. *A.U.,* III, 316.

31. *Ibid.,* III, 162.

Gabham deachmhaidh ar ndána. 'I am a poet', he says in effect, 'who for a long time has been composing poems in honour of others. It is now past time for me to pay a tithe of my works to God, to compose a poem in honour of him to whom I owe my art.'[32] An idea set forth by him and many another Irish poet was our strong claims to Mary's intercession because of our blood kinship with her. Sometimes this is developed to a paradoxical degree:

Tabhradh Mac ar seathar sinn
ar chionn éaga go hinill
rath críche gion go ndligh dhamh
ar na cíche ór ibh th'adhbhar

Dlighidh an Coimdhe rom chum
trócuire d'fhéachain oram
's é 'na dhearbhráthair 'n-a dhiaidh
deagh-mháthair Dé 'n-a deirbhshiair.[33]

About thirty poems of Pilib Bocht, with an average of about forty quatrains in each, have survived.[34] He was a Franciscan concerning whom few details have come down to us. His poems treat of Our Lady, the apostles, the saints (including St Patrick, St Dominic, and St Francis), the cross of Christ, God's mercy, the last judgment, bearing with our tribulations, and forgiving so that we may be forgiven. He shows himself more expert in the rules of metrics than in

32. M'Kenna (ed.), *Dán Dé*, Dublin [1922], 46-51.
33. *Ibid., 49:* May the son of you, my sister,
Bring me safely through life—
Though I do not deserve a good end—
You from whose breast He drank your substance.

The Lord who formed me
Must look mercifully on me;
After all, He is my brother
Since I have the good mother of God for a sister.

34. Ed. McKenna, in *Philip Bocht O Huiginn*, Dublin 1931. For another poem attributed to him see Mac Cionnaith (ed.), *Dioghluim dána*, Dublin 1938, 172-6.

theology. His compositions are stylized but musical, and he conjures up a number of striking images. In one of his poems on Our Lady he expresses regret that it was not she, the brown-haired, fair-toothed one, who was the first woman instead of Eve. Like Donnchadh Mór, he too pays a tithe on his poetry by composing a special poem in honour of Mary's Son. In another poem, he muses about heaven:

Annamh téid a-nonn a-nos
don lucht as lugha eolas
teirce do chách fear feasa
ar neamh is fáth faitcheasa.[35]

His poem on the last judgment, *Tuar feirge foighide Dé,* 'A presage of anger is God's patience', has the distinction of being the first printed work in Irish.

Tadhg Óg is the third of the outstanding poets we have mentioned. He composed both secular and religious poems, among the latter being ones in honour of Our Lady, St Michael, St John the Baptist, St Dominic, and other poems on the cross of Christ, the anger of God, heaven, and on leading a good life.

Other authors of religious poems were Seán Mór Ó Dubhagáin (O'Duggan), who died in 1374; Gofraidh Fionn Ó Dálaigh (O'Daly), who died in 1387; Tuathal Ó hUiginn (O'Higgins), who is probably to be identified with the person of that name who died in 1450; Cormac Rua Ó hUiginn, who flourished probably in the fourteenth or fifteenth century; and Risteard Buitléar or Richard Butler, who lived about the fifteenth or sixteenth century.

To Ó Dubhagáin is attributed a poem or series of poems on the feasts of the Church, and to Tuathal Óh Uiginn poems on the worthy reception of the Eucharist and on God's love

---

35. McKenna, *Philip Bocht O Huiginn,* 77:
       Seldom now go from here
       The folk of sparse knowledge
       But there rarest of all, I fear,
       Is the man of learning.

for men. Ó Dálaigh composed a poem beginning *Mairg mheallas muirn an tsaoghail,* 'Woe betide whom the love of the world beguiles.'

Butler is engaging, first, as an example of one of colonial stock turning his attention to Gaelic metre, and secondly, for the feel of his poetry. He redeems his lack of the technical skill of the earlier poets by a moving sincerity and spontaneity of which they rarely seemed capable. Two poems of his were written in illness:

> Rí in Domhnaigh mo dhochtúir-si
> is Muire liaigh dom leighis
> 's a chroch naemh gan rothuirsi
> go sgaraid mhé rem theinnis.[36]

Not improbably, he is also the author of a long poem of forty-seven quatrains on the power of Jesus.[37] On the very day he died, he composed a poem in praise of Jesus:

> Gidhbé gráidhis Ísa
> na chroidhi go cluthair
> ní théid aen grádh ele
> ann gu dere in domhain.[38]

There was no scarcity of devotional reading matter in Irish for the period from the invasion to the reformation, and nearly every new generation furnished its own quota. The

---

36. See Mac Niocaill, 'Dhá dhán le Risteard Buitléir', in *Éigse* 9, 83-8:
    May the King of Sunday, my doctor,
    And Mary, my physician in my illness—
    And the holy cross—grant, that without too great sorrow
    I shall be parted from my illness.

37. See *B.M. cat. Ir. MSS*, II, 496.

38. See Flower, *The Irish tradition,* 134-7:
    Whosoever loves Jesus
    In his heart contentedly,
    No other love possesses
    Till the world's end.

desirability of originality was not keenly felt. The need to make the available material more available still, by translation and transcription, was fully realized. For us, too, the translations and the modernizations have their value. They are useful pointers to the likes and dislikes, the hopes and fears, of the Irish speakers of the late medieval period. They all became formative elements of Irish spirituality.

Considering all this devotional literature globally – the prose and the poetry, the original compositions, the retellings from old Irish, and the adaptations from Latin and English – we can notice a stress on certain themes and deliberate neglect of others, the occurrence of some striking concepts, and the introduction of certain conceits from the apocryphal gospels, heathen folklore and Celtic mythology.

Themes of most frequent occurrence are the terrors of doomsday, the joys of heaven, the punishments of hell, the triviality of earthly glory in comparison with the eternal bliss to come, the omnipotence of God, the beauty, physical as well as spiritual, of Mary, and her great influence with her divine Son. The birth, infancy, last supper, passion and death of Christ are treated of at length and in detail, but the rest of his public life is practically ignored. References to purgatory are surprisingly rare, and one gets the impression at times that there is a confusion between the concepts of purgatory and hell. There is special devotion to St Michael and to the guardian angels, to the two St Johns, and to the three women saints, Mary Magdalene, Margaret of Antioch, and Catherine of Alexandria. The cross of our redemption, the virgin birth, the assumption of Our Lady, the real presence of Christ in the Eucharist, the sacrament of penance, and worthy preparation for the last sacraments, are mentioned frequently. The struggle for the mastery between man's soul and body is the theme of a number of prose and metrical compositions. Asceticism, fasting, pilgrimages, almsgiving, support of one's pastors, respect for the saints, their relics and termons, are all earnestly commended.

There are certain recurring concepts that do not appear to have been borrowed from abroad, although one cannot be categorical in such a matter. Life is compared to a hosting or foray against the world, the flesh, and the devil. Our obligations to God are represented as tithes and assessments. Christ's crucifixion for our sakes is spoken of in terms borrowed from the brehon laws as the payment of the eric or blood-fine. The description of his cross, or, as in some texts, of his body, as the charter of the peace re-established between God and man, though an Irish favourite, does not appear to have originated here. The consideration of Mary as our blood-relation and kinswoman is not a particularly Irish concept, but the peculiar elaboration of it to be found in Irish poetry almost certainly is. Lack of theological training and love of paradox and word-weaving led the poets into some daring and less orthodox modes of expression, and there are occasional turns of phrase that would not commend themselves to modern good taste.

Just as *Mór is Muire duit*, a combination of mythology and the Catholic faith, survives on the lips of present-day Irish speakers, and as the pagan *In ainm Chroim* alternates with the Christian *In ainm Dé,* so the medieval Irishman stood confused occasionally between his ancient heathen inheritance and the newer religion he had adopted. Some of those customs and beliefs will be treated of in the succeeding section. Here we are concerned only with those witnessed to in the literature.

The Christian ideal of the saint endued itself with some of the attributes of the heroes of Celtic mythology. St Brigid of Kildare acquired some of the gifts and magic of the three Brigid goddesses of the *Tuatha Dé Danaan.* Holy men were above all those who could work wonders at the upraising of a finger and to whom the future was as the present. Their feats of asceticism recalled the endurance tests of the *Fianna.* The angels took over some of the more benevolent functions of the fairies, and heaven was thought of as a Christian *Tír-na-nÓg,* the Land of Eternal Youth.

Apocryphal and legendary elements became inextricably intertwined with orthodox beliefs. There are certain signs that accompanied Christ's birth and certain signs that will precede the day of judgment. The soldier who pierced the side of Christ was blind, *An Dall,* and the 'ever-living' tongue of St Philip, *An teanga bithnua,* no matter how often it was cut out, had the power of perpetually renewing itself. There was a vogue in prophecies that were falsely fathered on the saints, and, to increase their semblance of credibility, descriptions in obscure terms of recent outstanding events were constantly being added to them. Heaven was a paradise of delightful bird-songs and had seven mansions. Hell was at once a place of scarifying heat and of icy cold. While heaven was above the clouds, hell was situated in the bowels of the earth with entrances to it by caves or pits in various parts of the world, of which Lough Derg was the most famous. Hell was conceived of as a place where the damned could gain temporary respite through the intercession of the angels and saints. This theme occurs not merely in the *Visio Sancti Pauli* and the *Dormitio Mariae,* two translated texts already mentioned, but also in the life of St Brendan of Clonfert, a text going back to the early Irish period.

A peculiar fancy was the Irish sense of responsibility for the killing of St John the Baptist. According to one account, the actual executioner was an Irish magician, Mogh Roith, a disciple of Simon Magus. There was a widespread belief that his death would be avenged by a calamitous phenomenon, such as a dreadful plague, which would sweep over Ireland for three days and nights some time before the end of the world. This was spoken of as *An Scuab a Fánaid,* 'The Broom out of Fána'. In the year 1096 panic seized the men of Ireland, and the Broom was believed to be imminent, but clergy and people undertook a total fast for three days of every week until the end of the year. That year passed without any untoward visitation, but 'The Broom out of Fána' continued for centuries to be spoken of and written of with awe.[39]

39. Grosjean, 'Le Balai de Fánaid', in *Études Celtiques* 2, 284-6; Müller-Lisowski, 'La légende de St Jean dans la tradition irlandaise et le druide Mog Ruith', in *Études Celtiques* 3, 46-70; Kenney, *Sources,* 279-80, 463, 703, 749-52.

SOME PARTICULAR CUSTOMS AND BELIEFS

Pilgrimages of all kinds were common, to shrines, churches, holy wells – and not merely to places near at hand, but to those at a distance. Among Irish places of pilgrimage mentioned in the annals and other sources are Derry, Raphoe, Boyle, Ballintubber, Clonfert, Cloyne, Cork, Ardmore, Kildare, Glendalough, Clonard, St Mullins, and, of course, Armagh, Clonmacnois, Lough Derg, and Croagh Patrick. Iona was also visited. The three great shrines of Christendom, Jerusalem, Rome, and Santiago di Compostela, were all much frequented by Irish pilgrims.

The *Annals of Loch Cé* and the *Annals of Connacht* tell of pilgrimages to Jerusalem and the River Jordan by Aodh, son of Conchobhar Maenmhaighe in 1224, by Ualgharg O'Rourke, king of Breffny, in 1231, and by Maol-Mhuire O'Lachtnáin, archbishop of Tuam, in 1249. By the year 1413 Giolla-Chríost Ó Fearadhaigh had already visited Rome and other shrines five times and was then about to set out for the Holy Sepulchre.[1] Two thirteenth-century poets, Muiríoch Albanach Ó Dálaigh of co. Sligo and Giolla-Brighde Mac Conmhidhe of Ulster, have left poems in Irish written in the Mediterranean while on pilgrimage to the holy places.[2]

Pilgrimages to Rome and Santiago were more frequent still. Exceptionally large numbers set out for Rome in the jubilee years of 1300, 1350, 1390, 1423, 1450, 1475, and 1500, and for Santiago during 1445 and 1462, which were years of special indulgence there. Owing to the perils of the time many died on the way. Donnchad, last surviving son of Brian Boruma, though the best known, is only one of many Irish pilgrims who left their bones in Rome. The journey took a long time. Thomas Maguire left Fermanagh on his pilgrimage to Rome 'a month after Lammas' in the year 1450

---

1. Lawlor (ed.), 'A calendar of the register of Archbishop Fleming', in *R.I.A. Proc.* 30, sect. C, 158 (no. 229).
2. See *B.M. cat. Ir. MSS,* I, 335-8.

and did not return until the beginning of the following year.[3] Aodh or Hugh O'Donnell, lord of Tyrconnell and north Connacht, set out for Rome in 1510 and did not reach home again until a year and a half later.[4]

From ancient down to modern times there has been a strong Irish belief in the value of fast and abstinence as a supererogatory ascetical practice and this went hand in hand with a certain rigidity in interpreting the rules regulating the official fasts of the Church. The lives of the Irish saints contain many examples of fasting carried to extreme lengths. The older literature speaks of three fasts in the year: that of Elias in Advent, of Christ in Lent, and of Moses following Pentecost. A homily occurring in several fifteenth-century manuscripts discusses profitable and unprofitable fasting.[5] A eulogy of Máire Ní Mháille (ob. 1522), wife of Rory MacSwiney of Tyrconnell, describes her as fasting three days in each week on bread and water as well as during the Lenten fast and the Advent fast and on the Twelve Golden Fridays.[6]

A less laudable use of fasting appears to be a survival from pagan times. That is the practice of *fasting against someone* or of *fasting on someone*. It was a form of moral coercion. A manuscript written partly in the fifteenth, partly in the sixteenth century, contains a story called *Mír do Mhícheál*, or 'Michael's Bit'. It describes a quarrel between St Patrick and King Laoire in which Patrick fasted against Laoire, and Laoire's son died because he had the temerity to go on eating while Patrick fasted.[7] In the fifteenth-century *Book of Lismore* occurs a story about a cleric fasting against God because he thought he had been unjustly treated.[8] But

---

3. *A.U.*, III, 164, 170.

4. *A.U.* III, 494, 496; *Ann. Conn.*, 1510, 7; 1512, 2.

5. See Atkinson (ed.), *The passions and homilies from the Leabhar Breac*, 274-5.

6. *Leabhar Clainne Shuibhne*, ed. Walsh, 67.

7. B.M., Add. MS 30512, f. 10. Also in Bodleian MS Rawl. B 512, from which it has been printed, with English translation, by Stokes, *The tripartite life of Patrick*, II, 556-9.

8. See Stokes (ed.), *Lives of saints from the Book of Lismore*, p. ix.

it was more than a mere literary motif. The clergy of Connacht fasted against Turloch O'Connor in 1144,[9] and a group of clerics of Armagh against Niall O'Neill in 1530,[10] and Magrath of the Termon against Failghe and Mellaghlin O'Neill in 1536.[11]

The practice of doughty warriors of taking out insurance against the terrors of the life to come by electing to be buried in the habit of some religious order is attested by many examples in the annals. Cathal Cróbhdhearg O'Connor, king of Connacht (ob. 1224), Cormac MacDermott, king of Clann Maol-Ruanaidh (ob. 1244), Donal O'Kelly, king of Uí Máine (ob. 1295), Aodh O'Donnell, king of Tyrconnell (ob. 1333), and Dermot Rua MacDermott (ob. 1342), all died in the habit of the Cistercian Order. Felim O'Connor (ob. 1448), died in the habit of St Dominic. Donal Óg MacSwiney Fanad, chief of his name (ob. 1528), assumed the Carmelite habit. Menelaus MacCormacan, bishop of Raphoe (ob. 1515), Eoghan O'Rourke, chieftain of West Breffny (ob. 1528), and Aodh Dubh O'Donnell, chieftain of Tyrconnell (ob. 1537), all died in the Franciscan habit.[12] Some of these died in their own houses, some in the monasteries or friaries of the order whose habit they donned.

There was a special devotion to the native saints and to the relics associated with them. Much was expected of them, even in the way of temporal favours, and some customs bordered on the superstitious. It was a common belief that the *Cathach* or Battler of Colmcille, of Caillín, of Jarlath, and of Greallán, ensured victory by its presence on the battlefield, although historical facts belied the belief and *Cathach* sometimes stood over against *Cathach*. Bells belonging to the saints were rung threateningly against all encroachers on monastic rights and privileges. Water that had been poured into the bells of saints or over manuscripts attributed to them, was given as a cure to sick animals. The *bachall* or staff of a saint

---

9. *A.F.M.*, II, 1072.
10. Gwynn, *The medieval province of Armagh,* Dublin 1946, 203.
11. *A.U.*, III, 606.
12. *Ann. Conn.; A.U.;* MacFirbis's 'Annals', in *Misc. Ir. Arch. Soc.,* I.

was feared and honoured because of the many miraculous tales narrated about its prowess. Woe to him who outraged the saints by violating their sanctuary or breaking a promise made over their relics. The annals contain many dire examples of what they considered as the vengeance of the saints. Yet, concomitant with this awe where wrong-doing was concerned went an easy familiarity of address and approach. Their heavenly patrons were simply Patrick, Brigid, Colman, and Canice, without title, and many saints became better known by pet-names and affectionate diminutives. Later generations unversed in this Gaelic usage found it difficult to grasp that pairs of seemingly different names like Aidan and Mogue, Mo-Laisse and Laserian, Ernóg and Marnock, Enan and Winoc, really designated one and the same person.

Paganism dies hard, and the older faiths leave many traces in the religion that succeeds them. Sacred wells were de-heathenized in the fifth and sixth centuries, but a thousand years later one encounters attitudes towards them among the people that savour more of paganism than Christianity. Relics of the saints are looked on by some of the uneducated as objects of magical power. Learned scribes of the fourteenth century will write pagan charms into their manuscripts just after a prayer to Christ or Our Lady. And let us see what the staid and sober pages of the annals have to reveal of the mentality of their times.

In the year 1411 the holy cross of Raphoe shed blood from its wounds,[13] and in 1482 a holy cross appeared on the margin of the lake of Baile-an-chuilinn and wrought many miracles and wonders.[14] True, possibly, but we should like verification, especially when we encounter such entries as the following: in 1414 the poet Niall Mór Ó hUiginn of Uisneach lampooned John Stanley for plundering him, and five weeks later Stanley died from the venom of the lampoons. Niall's other miracle, add the annals, was the freezing to death of the Clann-Conway on the night after they had plundered him in

---

13. *A.U.*, III, 60; *Ann. Conn.*, 1411, 24; *A.F.M.*, IV, 804.
14. *A.U.*, III, 280; *A.F.M.*, IV, 1118.

D

Clada, co. Galway, in the year 1400.[15] One of the outstanding leaders of his day, Tadhg O'Brien, king of Thomond, when at the height of his career, died of the lectual fever in 1466, and it was generally believed that he was killed by the evil eye.[16] A bizarre ritual, part pagan, part Christian, took place in 1277 when Brian Rua O'Brien and the son of the earl of Clare made gossipry with each other, mixed their blood in one vessel, and bound themselves to each other in friendship upon the relics of Munster and bells and croziers.[17] Reference has already been made to the vogue of forged prophecies. Those were usually ones of general import or even national interest, but the *Annals of Connacht* under the year 1282 mention, with evident credulity, one of a more personal nature. Cathal O'Farrell, chieftain of the Annaly, had been warned that he was fated to die on *An Iomaire Fada*, The Long Ridge. He always sedulously avoided it, but one day in 1282 he died on Inis Cuan at a place where there was a long ridge, *iomaire fada*, never suspecting that that was the long ridge which was destined to be 'the sod of his death'.[18] Around the years 1383–9 Archbishop Colton of Armagh issued provincial constitutions in which he condemned the superstitious belief that the blood of a hare on Good Friday was protection against and a remedy for various diseases. To put an end to the abuse, he forbade the hunting of any wild animal, but especially the hare, on that day.[19]

Heresy was a word that was bandied about as recklessly in medieval times to decry an opponent as communism is in some circles at present, but outbreaks of heresy in the strict sense were very rare in Ireland. Aduk or Adam Duff O'Toole was burned in 1326 at Hogges Green, Dublin, for blasphemy

15. *Ann. Conn.*, 1400, 13; 1414, 16.
16. *Ann. Conn.*, 1466, 14; Mac Firbis's 'Annals', in *Misc. Ir. Arch. Soc.*, I, 258-9.
17. *Ann. Conn.*, 1277, 2; *Ann. Clon.*, 251.
18. *Ann. Conn.*, 1282, 7.
19. *Acts of Archbishop Colton*, ed. Reeves, Ir. Arch. Soc., Dublin 1850, p. xvii. The translation in *The register of John Swayne*, Belfast 1935, ed. Chart, p. 11, is not very accurate.

and heresy. He was accused of having denied the incarnation, the Trinity, the resurrection of the dead, and the truth of the scriptures, and of having declared that Our Lady was a woman of dissolute life. He was alleged to have led many of the native Irish into error by his preaching before he was arrested.[20] In March 1256 the Pope granted permission to Patrick O'Scanlan, O.P., bishop of Raphoe, to proceed against certain laymen of his diocese who were worshipping idols and marrying within the forbidden degrees of affinity and consanguinity.[21] In 1353 Thomas de Rokeby, justiciary of Ireland, invaded Thomond in a campaign against the Irish, and on that occasion two of the MacNamara sept were convicted at Bunratty and burned for heresy, or, more precisely, for obscene contumely offered to Our Lady.[22] The outbreaks of heresy in Ossory and Dublin in 1324 and 1351, the case of the Cistercian, Henry Crump, and the process against the Knights Templar for heresy and other crimes did not concern the Church among the Irish.

In the Great Schism (1378–1417), a number of the clergy and laymen of Connacht gave their allegiance to Cardinal Robert of Geneva, the anti-pope Clement VII, and to his successors. Clement sent Thomas MacEgan, prior of the house of canons regular of St Augustine at Roscommon, as his emissary to Ireland, and Thomas secured the support of the archbishop of Tuam and the bishops of Kilmacduach, Clonfert, Achonry, and, as he claimed, other prelates as well, and a multitude of secular priests, regulars, and lay people, but he was opposed by Robert Eliot, bishop of Killala, and his archdeacon, John Mac Oireachtaigh. Clement suspended Robert and the bishop of Elphin, while, on the other hand, Pope Urban excommunicated the arch-

---

20. 'Littera ad Ioannem XXII, ed. Watt, in *I.H.S.* 10, 20 (March 1956); Dowling, 'Annales breves Hiberniae', 22, in Butler (ed.), *The annals of Ireland*, Ir. Arch. Soc., Dublin 1849.

21. Theiner, *Vetera mon.*, 71; *Cal. papal letters*, I, 329.

22. Fitzmaurice and Little, *Franciscan province Ire.*, 144; Wadding, *Annales Minorum*, VIII, 124; Gleeson, 'A fourteenth-century Clare heresy trial', in *I.E.R.* (series 5) 89, 36-42 (Jan. 1958).

bishop of Tuam, and Pope Boniface condemned Thomas MacEgan. Outside of the Tuam province, the anti-popes received a certain amount of support in the dioceses of Cashel, Armagh, Clogher, and Raphoe.

During the reign of the anti-pope Clement, three of the Irish archbishoprics fell vacant, and he made provisions to all three, none of which proved very successful. He also provided several other Irishmen to benefices and granted indulgences and dispensations to a number of Connacht clerics and laypeople who journeyed to Avignon in 1379.[23]

ABUSES AND INDISCIPLINE

While the abuse of lay appropriation of church lands during the earlier period eventually regularized itself into the accepted system of coarbs, erenaghs, and *dúchasaigh*, later times saw new encroachments, undertaken either suddenly and with violence, or subtly and with calculated insistence. The excuse proffered might be that the chieftain needed the monastic land for the defence of his territory, or that so much land was no longer needed by a diminished community, or that there was no good reason for allowing such valuable episcopal lands to pass into the hands of an English absentee, or that an Irish chieftain was as entitled as an English king to take the fruits of a see during the vacancy. Other ways in which church property passed into lay hands were simoniacal bargaining by rival claimants, alienation because of poverty or loose living, usurpation by an illegitimate son of the previous holder, and reluctance by long-settled farmers to acknowledge the church as the true owner.

Associated evils were lay patronage and interference, which often led to the appointment of less worthy candidates. Builders of churches, owners of lands bequeathed to the

23. *Cal. papal letters*, IV, 245-6, 340, 348, 442-3; *Cal. papal petitions*, 541-2, 556, 559. For a more detailed account of the effects of the Schism in Ireland see ch. IV (Gwynn, 'Anglo-Irish Church life: fourteenth and fifteenth centuries', 51 ff.).

church, and their heirs sought the right to nominate their own candidates as rector or vicar. Powerful chieftains, as, for example, O'Neill, O'Donnell and Maguire, towards the end of our period, emulous of other Christian princes, claimed various rights of advowsons, patronage, and presentation to churches within their territory. The papal registers reveal what a large number of Irish benefices in the fifteenth century were even acknowledged at Rome as of lay patronage, and occasionally they give illuminating insights into the dubious origins of some of these claims.

Sporadic examples of disregard for churches and church property are to be found in all ages in Ireland, but they became particularly prevalent during certain periods of unrest. About 1330 the Irish of Leinster were accused of having burned 340 churches.[1] About 1377 a large amount of ecclesiastical property was pillaged or destroyed in the diocese of Emly.[2] In 1407 died Hugh MacGilmurry or MacGilmor, who was reputed to have destroyed forty churches in north and east Ulster.[3] These all appear to have been part of different ruthless campaigns to drive out the English. There are other examples of deliberate church burnings where the motive was plunder, to kill an enemy trapped inside, or even sheer revenge, as when Felim O'Mellaghlin with his followers plundered the cathedral and monastery of Clonfert in 1541 to avenge the plunder of the houses and churches of Tisaxon, Offaly, by the sons of O'Madden.[4] On several occasions men were slain by their enemies inside a church. We know of at least one occasion on which a church was used as cover for an ambushing party. Cattle, sheep, horses, and corn, were often taken unlawfully from church lands.

Nor did the persons and personal property of the clergy always go safe. The bishop of Derry was robbed on his way

1. 'Littera ad Ioannem XXII', ed. Watt, in *I.H.S.* 10, 19 (March 1956).
2. Theiner, *Vetera mon.*, 358-60.
3. Dowling, 'Annales breves Hiberniae,' 26.
4. *A.F.M.*, V, 1460.

to Armagh in 1442,[5] and the bishop of Killala was killed in 1461.[6] The greatest mass slaughter of Irish clerics was when Conor O'Neill and the Cenéal Eoghain killed sixteen of the principal clergy of the Cenéal Conaill at Derry in 1261.[7] There are examples to show that the clergy were not always above returning blow for blow, as when Eugene O'Fahy, prior of Aughrim, co. Galway, betrayed by drink and anger, killed a layman of the diocese of Clonfert with a single stroke of a sword in 1470.[8] Sometimes it was cleric against cleric, as when Maurice MacMurrough Cavanagh, archdeacon of Leighlin, killed Maurice O'Doran, his bishop, on the public road in the autumn of 1525.[9]

References to members of the clergy taking part in armed forays and warlike acts are not infrequent. The bishop of Clonmacnois, Cormac or Cornelius MacCoughlan, and his son James, archdeacon of the diocese, and the prior of Clontuskert, were slain in 1444 in a battle with another sept of the MacCoughlans. Far from the bishop being a peace-lover, it was he who would not tolerate any talk of cessation of hostilities.[10] The bishop of Ardagh, William O'Farrell, took Rory O'Farrell, joint chief of the Annaly, prisoner in 1496 and soon after had himself proclaimed O'Farrell.[11] Turloch O'Brien, bishop of Killaloe, who died in 1525, is described as a man for defending his rights at home and abroad, with or without consent, and a man for frequently setting large armies against each other in order to destroy his enemies.[12]

The poverty of many Irish benefices, which in itself was often partially due to remediable factors like mismanagement

5. Prene's register, in Reeves (ed.), *Acts of Archbishop Colton*, 11-12, footnotes.

6. *Ann. Conn.*, 1461, 11; MacFirbis's 'Annals', in *Misc. Ir. Arch. Soc.*, 243.

7. *A.U.*, II, 328, 330; *Ann. Conn.*, 1261, 2; *A.L.C*, I, 436, 438; *A.F.M.*, III, 380.

8. *Cal. papal letters*, XII, 768.

9. Dowling, 'Annales breves Hiberniae', 34; *A.L.C.*, II, 250, 252.

10. MacFirbis's 'Annals', in *Misc. Ir. Arch. Soc.*, 204-5.

11. *A.U.*, III, 402; *Ann. Conn.*, 1516, 7.

12. *A.L.C.*, II, 252; *Ann. Conn.*, 1525, 5; *A.U.*, III, 558.

and civil strife, begot a numerous and evil progeny – pluralism, non-residence, neglect of divine service, dilapidation, a lowering of standards for candidates to the priesthood, and clerical engagement in the trades and professions.

David O'Donir of Killaloe diocese was provided to a canonry in 1343 with expectation of a prebend, notwithstanding that he already had canonries of Cashel and Cloyne, a certain rectory, and the vicarage of Clogher, co. Tipperary.[13] That was a fairly typical example of pluralism. Many bishops were non-resident because they had found it pleasanter and more profitable to go as suffragans or auxiliaries to some English bishop. About the year 1432 there were no less than four men claiming to be bishop of the poverty-stricken diocese of Dromore, and all four were residing in England. In all, we find about nine bishops of Dromore, and as many more from Annadown, in pre-reformation times acting as suffragans in England and Wales. There were, besides, about four from Achonry, three from Clonfert, and three from Killala. Many an Englishman appointed to a penurious Irish diocese never even bothered to pay it a visit. Before the end of the fifteenth century the communities of several priories of canons regular had ceased to live together. They acquired their own little portions of land and separate habitations. In some cases, the priories were monopolized by the prior or a few canons or had already passed into lay hands. Finally, in regard to engagement in trades and professions, Denis or Donnchadh MacInerney, a cleric of Killaloe, was practising the art of medicine for profit in 1399,[14] Eugene Ó Faoláin, a cleric of Cloyne and a bachelor of laws, was in 1484 trafficking in salt, iron, and other merchandise and teaching in schools of civil law,[15] while Matthew O'Mulryan, abbot of Holy Cross about 1490, was carrying on a trade in wine, and often getting drunk in the process.[16]

13. *Cal. papal letters*, III, 100.
14. *Cal. papal letters*, V, 315.
15. *Cal. papal letters*, XIII, 162-3.
16. *Cal. papal letters*, XIV, 224-6, 254-7.

The Irish chieftains were given to much marrying. Take the O'Donnells of Tyrconnell, for example. Mellaghlin (ob. 1247) and Dónal Óg (ob. 1281) had each at least four wives; Dónal's son Aodh (ob. 1333) had at least five; Turloch of the Wine (ob. 1422) had ten; Neachtan (ob. 1452) had six; and Aodh Dubh (ob. 1537) had four.[17] It is hardly to be presumed that wives in those days were dying off so rapidly, especially since it was common practice for middle-aged men to marry very young girls, and there are other examples to show that men did often put away their wives and take another woman into the house. This was done, sometimes for love or lust, sometimes for political motives. Examples of much-married women are Gormliath MacDermott (ob. 1327) and Cabhlaigh Mór O'Connor (ob. 1395). Gormliath was married first to Manus O'Connor, then to Conor O'Kelly, and then to Fearghal O'Hara.[18] Cabhlaigh, who was a daughter of the king of Connacht, was facetiously nicknamed *Port-na-dtrí-namhad*, 'The Haven of the Three Enemies', after a Tyrconnell placename because she married three warriors who were sworn enemies. Nor were those her only consorts.[19] The tendency to marriage within the forbidden degrees of consanguinity and affinity gave colour to the English accusations of incest against the Irish.

Concubinage was also common, and in this regard not merely laymen but the clergy stand convicted. Among the statutes of a provincial synod of Armagh around the period 1383–9 was one against lay or clerical subjects of Armagh holding women as concubines under the name of 'cayf' (from Irish *caomh*) or 'chogir' (from Irish *cogar* or *bean chogair*).[20] Provincial statutes of Cashel in the fifteenth century ordered concubines to be put away within a month of the promulgation of the decrees in the different dioceses.[21]

17. See Walsh (ed.), 'O'Donnell genealogies', in *Anal. Hib.* 8, 373-418, or Pender (ed.), 'The O Clery book of genealogies', in *Anal. Hib.* 18, 5-14.
18. *Ann. Conn.*, 1327, 3; *A.L.C.*, I, 604, 606.
19. *A.U.*, III, 30.
20. Chart (ed.), *The register of John Swayne*, 11.
21. *Cal. papal letters*, XII, 637; XIII, 394.

We are told that when Archbishop Colton went on visitation to Derry in 1397 he insisted on the abbot of Derry dismissing his concubine, Catherine O'Doherty, and forbade the canons to introduce any woman of suspicious character into the abbey, or to allow her to sleep there.[22]

No rank of the secular clergy, no religious order, not even cloistered nuns, were without blame. Surnames like *Mac an tSagairt, Mac an Phríóir, Mac an Mháighistir, Mac an Déagánaigh, Mac an Easpaig,* as well as designations in the annals like *Clann an Easpaig Uí Ghallachair, Mac an Abaidh Óig, Mac an Archdeochain Mhóir,* all tell their own tale. The number of candidates for ecclesiastical office from Ireland who had first to seek dispensation from illegitimacy is far greater than the numbers from England, Scotland, or Wales.

Let us illustrate the position with some examples from the higher ranks of the clergy. Art MacCawell, bishop of Clogher, who died in 1432, had at least five children, some, if not all, of whom were by a woman related to him sixfold by affinity, and of whom some at least were born after he was made bishop. One son became rector of Aghalurcher and canon of Clogher. Of his great-grandsons, one became dean of Clogher, and another its bishop. A daughter of his 'married' Maurice Maguire, known as 'The Great Archdeacon', who in turn had a numerous progeny. One of Maurice's sons, Pierce or Peter, born when his father was already a priest, became bishop of Clogher in 1433; another, Thomas, became abbot of Lisgoole; and a third, John, became prior of Devenish. Abbot Thomas took Anne MacCabe as his mistress and had several children by her. Bishop Pierce had at least four sons, all of whom held ecclesiastical offices. Edmond became archdeacon, Turloch a choral canon and also prior of Lough Derg, and William abbot of Lisgoole. William was the father of at least four sons. Prior John of Devenish, mentioned above, was in turn the father of Seán Cam, parson of Collooney. Archbishop Edmond, son of Bishop Pierce, was in his turn the father of Réamann, vicar

22. Reeves (ed.), *Acts of Archbishop Colton,* 57.

of Cleenish, and of a daughter Finnuala, who married the head of the O'Breslin sept. Thomas Óg Maguire, king of Fermanagh, who died in 1480, had an illegitimate son, Ros or Roger, who became bishop of Clogher in 1447, and who was the father of at least ten children. Following the established tradition, many of them were granted church livings. Cathal Óg MacManus Maguire, chief compiler of the *Annals of Ulster*, who died in 1498, canon choral of both Armagh and Clogher, dean of the rural deanery of Lough Erne, and parson of Inishkeen, had a very large family, some of whom were born after he became canon of Clogher, and some more after he became dean of Lough Erne. One of his sons, Thomas, a cleric, married Siobhán, daughter of Andrew MacBrady, bishop of Kilmore.

We find the pattern repeating itself in other dioceses. Richard O'Reilly, bishop of Kilmore from 1356 to 1369, had four sons and was living over a long period adulterously and incestuously with Éadaoin O'Reilly and also cohabiting with another relative, Éadaoin Magauran. Lawrence or Lorcan O'Gallagher, bishop of Raphoe from 1442 to 1479, was the illegitimate son of Donal, who was the illegitimate son of the second last bishop, another Lawrence O'Gallagher, who was the grandson of a monk. The second Bishop Lawrence had at least six sons, several of whom became clerics. One of them, Brian, had an illegitimate son Éamann, who became bishop of the diocese in 1534. Thomas O'Flanagan, a priest of the diocese of Elphin, was the son of Donal, provost of the diocese, who was the son of Nicholas O'Flanagan, O.P., who was appointed bishop in 1458, and who was the illegitimate son of Dermot Carrach. Donal was born when his father was already a bishop, and his mother, a married woman, appears to have been one of the MacEgan family. The Great Dean O'Farrell, a priest at the time, was father of Richard O'Farrell, O.Cist., bishop of Ardagh from 1425 to 1444, and of Seán or John, abbot of Abbeylara. James O'Farrell, another abbot of Abbeylara, was a son of Bishop Richard. Cormac Magauran, who became bishop of Ardagh in 1444, was the illegitimate son of Peter Magauran, a canon regular of St Augustine, and the father of the Cormac Magauran who became bishop of Kilmore in 1476. The second Cormac was born when the first Cormac was already a priest. Ralph O'Kelly, archbishop of Cashel, who died in 1361, was the illegitimate son by the wife of William O'Kelly, a Drogheda merchant, of the most celebrated Irish Carmelite in pre-reformation times, David O'Buge (a form, perhaps, of the Irish name Mac Giolla Buidhe). In 1475 Edmond O'Hedian of Emly and Thomas O'Tombaigh of Kilfenora were enjoying ecclesiastical benefices granted to them by the bishops of those two dioceses, but in each case the bishop was the father of the beneficiary.[23]

Little or no social stigma attached to concubinage or illegitimacy. Abbots and bishops often took as their concubines the sisters and daughters of the local chiefs and of eminent scholars. Their illegitimate offspring married or consorted with members of the best families in the district. The decline in discipline had been so widespread that many clerical offenders must have salved their consciences with the persuasion that the old statutes had ceased to bind and that they were guilty at most of a mere technical or legal offence. The existence of a class who were clerics, with or without minor orders, yet validly married; the blurring of many of the distinctions between cleric and layman; the growing tendency to merge civil and ecclesiastical offices; all those factors added to the confusion in the popular mind. The general laxity all over Europe in the century or two preceding the reformation and the bad example from on high helped to stifle the consciousness of wrong-doing. The Bishop Art MacCawell, whom we have mentioned as the father of five children, is praised by the annalists as a man of hospitality and piety.[24] Cathal Óg MacManus Maguire, a cleric we have referred to as being the father of over a dozen children, is lauded in the continuation of the annals he helped to compile,

---

23. The preceding two paragraphs were compiled from data in the annals, the Armagh registers, the Irish genealogical tracts, Ware's *Bishops,* and *Cal. papal letters.*
24. *A.U.,* III, 122.

not merely for his high offices and hospitality and scholarly
attainments – that, we can readily endorse – but also – and
here a certain puzzlement possesses us – as a gem of purity
and a turtle-dove of chastity![25]

Councils, synods, visitations, and various forms of
disciplinary action were all invoked from time to time by
conscientious prelates and superiors to recall delinquent
clergy to a sense of duty, but the rot had gone deep and the
spirit of the time was opposed to moral reform. It was only
when the unity of western Christendom had already been
tragically shattered that an effective reform movement,
based on careful selection and proper training of candidates,
was finally launched.

The Anglo-Norman invasion brought problems in its train
for the Church in Ireland that would surely have given pause,
could they only have foreseen them, to the Irish prelates
who so light-heartedly promised allegiance to King Henry II
at Cashel in 1171. Racial and political cleavages bedevilled
ecclesiastical administration, especially in regard to such
matters as appointments, elections, visitations, finance, and
disciplinary actions. It was not always easy for an Anglo-
Norman archbishop to obtain his services and cesses from
his Irish clergy and people, or for an English religious
superior to go on visitation to the Irish districts and enforce
an unpopular judgment against a delinquent Irish priest or
religious.

On the other hand, the Irish cleric had his own grievances.
The English authorities in the country, ecclesiastical as well
as civil, tended to regard him with a jaundiced eye. The
scales were loaded against his chances of promotion, except
in the wilder and poorer districts and when there was no
rival English candidate of even average ability. If he did
happen to have an Englishman under his authority, any
reprimand administered to him for his misdemeanours

25. *A.U.*, III, 428, 430.

might be represented as felonious infringement of the rights
of one of the king's loyal subjects.

We have seen that the economic and educational organization of the *ecclesia inter Hibernos* was of a kind hardly to be
found anywhere else in Christendom. Yet, given normal
social conditions and good will on all sides, it was capable of
producing good fruit. Hospitality, in the very widest sense
of that word, flourished almost to a fault. The poor and the
pilgrim, the wandering scholar, scribe, and harpist, all
found welcome, food, and lodging at the many houses of
hospitality that dotted the countryside. The sick poor, the
lepers (in the medieval sense) and the orphans were all fairly
adequately catered for. Despite the rigidly stratified nature
of Irish society, hardly any obstacle was placed in the way of
the advancement in Church or society of individuals of poor
or handicapped origins, provided they possessed ability and
character.

The Church among the Irish partook of a rural character,
as distinct from the rather 'urban' nature of the Church of
the Pale and the Anglo-Norman settlements. Towns were
few and small. Land, cattle and corn were the usual sources
of wealth. There was more barter and payment in kind. The
people were less sophisticated, more superstitious, more
conservative in customs and beliefs. There was little prostitu-
tion, hardly any sign of sexual aberrations, but perhaps
more concubinage and more marrying within the forbidden
degrees of kindred. There were no theatres, dramas, or
mystery plays. There was no creative literature. Preaching
and the liturgy were even more neglected than in the Anglo-
Irish towns. There was little regard for the preservation of
administrative records and registers or for their safe transfer
to successors in office.

Portrait painting was ignored, figure or narrative painting,
judging from surviving remains, had only a limited development. Music flourished as in few countries. There still
remain to us some examples of admirable workmanship in
stone, metal, and wood. Architecture reached its apogee,
in the form of Irish Gothic, in the century preceding the

reformation, but the late twelfth and early thirteenth centuries also saw the erection of a number of impressive churches and monasteries in the transitional style.

Devotional reading matter was abundant but consisted mainly of works in Latin by continental authors, translations into Irish of Latin and English prose texts, and a large amount of poetry, stylized and studied, of high technical skill, but not, as a rule, particularly emotive or evocative. The period of greatest literary activity was the fifteenth century.

Theft, robbery, and murder, do not seem to have been any more or less frequent than elsewhere at the same period. There was, however, a multiplicity of small wars, from which hardly any part of the country was immune, and which begot acts of violence in a variety of forms. Mutilation of captured political opponents was common practice. Standards of sexual morality left much to be desired, especially during the century or two before the reformation. Clerical celibacy was sharply on the decline. Alienation and dilapidation of church property were prevalent. Pluralism, absenteeism, neglect of church services, all appear to have been on the increase. A gleam of hope, apart from the exemplary living of many individual churchmen in a tainted atmosphere, was provided by the successful religious revival inaugurated by the Observant movement in the orders of friars and by the remarkable diffusion of the Third Order Regular in the west and north, but the suppression of the monasteries intervened before the whole mass could be leavened.